About the Authors

In February 2013, we left on our adventures. We were young, complete 4x4 dummies, totally unprepared, but entirely motivated to make a go of it. So on a cold, wintery morning, we got into our not-so-little Toyota Landcruiser and left our little home country of Belgium. We drove through Europe, took the ferry from Turkey to Egypt and started our journey along the East African coast towards South Africa.

Of course, there were many ups and downs. We got stuck in the middle of the Sudanese desert during our first week there. We had no idea how to use our hi-lift jack. We had to dismantle our beautiful fitted cupboard after just two months on the road (the one we worked so hard on, sorry Vake!). We had a major breakdown on the Lake Turkana route. We ran out of money after just eight months of travelling ...

However ...

... We also got to be guests at a Sudanese wedding, hiked up a live volcano, saw gorillas in the wild, swam in the bluest seas on Earth, rescued a cow from a ditch and scuba dived with manta rays. We met the most amazing people and made lifelong friends.

And then there are all the amazing memories we have and will have forever. There are the ways in which we've changed. It's hard for us to say exactly how, but our views on the world, our approach towards (strange) people, our ideas about contributing to society, our affinity with nature ... all have been affected by our travels in some way or another.

We know this book isn't set out like most of the overland books on the market, but our book hasn't solely been written in order to inform you about 4x4ing in Africa. There are plenty of choices out there for instruction manuals. Our book is not a textbook full of do's and don'ts. We won't advise you on which shock absorbers to buy, or which tyres to avoid. We write on a more personal level. We tell you about our personal experiences on the road, let you in on our first timer mistakes that so easily could have been avoided, but most of all, our goal is to encourage anyone who reads our book to throw themselves into this African adventure with all their hearts. Just like we did. But without making quite so many mistakes!

It took us two years to reach South Africa, after which we flew over to Australia, bought the same model of car (but in white, this time) and worked and travelled through Australia. Next was New Zealand, Papua New Guinea, Vietnam and today, as I write this, we're in Cambodia. Tomorrow we fly out to China to take the Trans-Siberian Express home after a four-year-long adventure.

We hope our book will help you prepare yourself for your future journey and, if you're not quite there yet, that it at least gives you the push you need to start planning your adventure.

Enjoy the Big Wide World!

Eef, Dries and Mr. Carrot.

Want to read more about our travels?

Have a look at our website. You will find more of our stories, pictures and travels at www.whereismistercarrot.com or you can follow us on Facebook www.facebook.com/waarisworteltje.

INTO AFRICA:
A PRACTICAL GUIDE TO 4x4ING ACROSS AFRICA

Contact: info@intoafrica.be

Visit the authors' website at: www.whereismistercarrot.com

Interior and cover design by Misha Gericke

INTO
Africa

A Practical Guide
to 4x4ing Across Africa

Eef Lenaerts and Dries Lembrechts

Contents

Introduction

Most of us don't travel across Africa every year; most of the time, it's a once-in-a-lifetime thing. A long journey requires a lot of preparation, a lot of expensive purchases, a lot of organisation, a lot of thought ... so where should you start?

Which type of vehicle is best? Will you need an extra diesel tank? What should you take? What shouldn't you take? What's going to be useful? Which documents need to be in order? The to-do list is endless.

You begin to read up. In the beginning, it's a lot of fun. You scroll through endless forums, order countless books, make initial plans and spend long evenings in front of a computer screen, reading about other people's travel experiences.

You are completely convinced that you want to do this, that you're going to do it, that you will soon be off on your adventures!

You tell your friends and family ... and watch as they frown.

And start asking questions ...

> Isn't Africa supposed to be dangerous?
> What will you do with your house?
> How will you earn money?
> What if you get ill?
> What happens if you get malaria?

Can your vehicle cope with the journey?
What if you get stuck somewhere; if you break down in the middle of the desert without any water?
Don't people get taken hostage over there?
What if ...? What if ...?

You'll hear all the second-hand stories ...

'My colleague's neighbour's sister's cousin went to Africa and caught malaria. He had to share a hospital ward with 50 other patients—they used one needle for every ten of them.'

'I read about someone who slept in a roof tent, and a lion climbed the ladder. They only found his body a month later.'

You'll hear their opinions ...

'Africa is so dangerous, don't go!'
'If you give up your job, you'll never get another one!'
'Don't sell your house now, the market's incredibly slow!'

But most of all, you will hear:

Africa is dangerous!
Africa is dangerous!
Africa is dangerous!

You probably expected at least some people to be less than enthusiastic about your plans, but hey, you're still enthusiastic, and you're still going!

So, you start getting ready. You buy bits of equipment and plan the start of your trip, buy some more gear and plan the next stage.

Your departure date looms ever closer, but you postpone it ... just a little. This later departure date begins to creep up on you and you postpone again.

You watch as your 'home' disappears into boxes. You look at your parents' worried faces. Your bank account gets emptier and emptier ...

And you're still saying to everyone, absolutely convinced: 'We're going! This is the best idea we ever had!' Exhaustion, stress and doubts fill your head.

> Will we find another job?
> Will our friends still be our friends when we get back?
> What if a family member gets ill?
> Will we have enough money?
> Is this really such a good idea?

To this last question, we always found ourselves answering a resounding 'YES!'

We went through all of this three years ago, but we can definitely say that making this journey was the best idea we ever had!

Of course, it's not all happy songs and rainbows. There will be rain, car trouble and bad days. However, these are nothing compared to the pure wealth of experiences, the friendships, the freedom, the passion out there waiting for you.

So all we can do is encourage you to take the plunge.

Sell your house, give up your job, throw all your possessions into boxes and start your adventure!

1

Where Do You Begin?

So, you've decided you want to make this trip. You're really excited, but then comes that all important question: where do you begin?

We also found this to be difficult; travelling all the way across Africa is not something one does every day, so there isn't that much information about it—

In fact, let us phrase that differently, there *is* a lot of information about, but just not in one spot.

We've done this trip and there are so many things that we learned along the way that we wish we had known before we left. We often came across something and thought: 'Really? Wish we had known that before we left home!' (It might also have something to do with the fact that we weren't very prepared and left in a mad rush.)

But anyway, this is the reason we have decided to write this book; to put everything we have learned and discovered via trial and error into one place, so that you can benefit from our hands-on experiences. We hope we have succeeded!

Research

Preparing for your trip will take a lot of research and reading. You will spend a lot of late nights behind your computer screen, often unable to stop when reading others' stories, letting their advice point you towards various research sources.

> *I ended up spending many, many hours behind the computer, becoming totally absorbed in other travelers' stories, looking at millions of pictures, watching their travel trailers. As soon as you start with your online research, it's like you're a kid in a sweet shop, and is completely addictive!*
> *—Eef*

Books

Africa Overland from Bradt

This book will help you start planning your trip and select the right vehicle. It also provides you with a rough estimate of the costs involved, includes a checklist of what to take and offers information about the red tape of each African country. We think this is a good book to start with, giving you a rough overall idea of what lies ahead.

Sahara Overland by Chris Scott

Chris Scott travelled through the Sahara for 35 years and was nice enough to share his knowledge with us. In this book, he gives planning and preparation information for travelling by car, bike and camel through the Saharan environment. As well as this, he also gives more specific information about travelling along the West Coast of Africa.

Overlanders' Handbook by Chris Scott

Another book by Chris Scott, but this time expanded to include the whole world.

Help for worldwide planning and routes for car, 4WD, van and truck. We didn't know this book existed, but going by the reviews, it's an overlander's bible!

Vehicle-Dependent Expedition Guide by Tom Sheppard and Jonathan Hanson

Apparently, this is the most detailed book on the subject of trip preparation (which is probably why the price is so high at US$75). The book is distributed in North-America, but you can't find the latest edition (the fourth edition) on Amazon.

You can buy the book on the 'Exploring Overland' website at www.exploringoverland.com/publications.

Motorhome Self-Built and Optimisation

Planning on (re)building your own overland truck? Ulrich built his own and travelled the world with it. In his book, he tells you how to build/upgrade your own truck/camper, including all the mistakes he has made on the way.

You can buy his (E-) book via Amazon or on his website at www.selfbuildmotorhome.com; it is published in both English and German.

Shifting into 4WD by Harry Lewellyn

This is a book for absolute beginners who have never driven a four-wheel-drive vehicle (4WD). It covers the basics and it helps you to understand what a 4WD actually is. It isn't the best book about 4WD's, as it doesn't cover muddy terrain or winch recovery etc., but it's an easy-to-read-book.

The book is written with a great sense of humour and we (as 4WD dummies) could fully understand what he was talking about, especially in comparison with other 4WD books. So although it's not the 4WD bible, it's a great place to start for dummies.

Four-by-Four Driving by Tom Sheppard
Another book by Tom Sheppard (and distributed in North America). You can find it on the Exploring Overland website at www.exploringoverland.com.

Travel Guides
It goes without saying that travel guides will give you more info about the country and the culture.

Lonely Planet and **Bradt** have some pretty good ones.

We preferred Bradt, as Lonely Planet seems to be more focused on backpackers. Bradt has more information relating to campsites.

However, we preferred the Lonely Planet maps to those included in the Bradt guides, as they provided us with a nice overview on what to see and where to find it. The choice is yours.

Leisure
Many overlanders have written books about their adventures. (Overland by bike, by 4WD, with kids, in a tractor, etc.) Just type the words 'overland' or 'overland adventure' in the Amazon search engine and you're off!

Magazines
Overland Journal
www.overlandjournal.com

Overland Journal is published five times a year and provides in-depth coverage of equipment and vehicles. It contains some very interesting stories about overlanders from all over the world. Together with stunning photography, this is a very pleasant read.

Overland Magazine
www.overlandmag.com

This magazine is focused on overlanding for motorcycles and is for sale in the UK, Ireland and the USA. You can also find more information about overlanding with your motorcycle, info about insurance, choosing the right bike etc. on their website.

Websites
Exploring Overland
www.exploringoverland.com

These two American guys share their extensive knowledge with you. On their website, you will find tips and tricks, as well as stories about their adventures.

They also host expos and some training sessions; interesting to check out if you live in the US.

Overlanding Association
www.overlandingassociation.org

You can find a lot of useful information on this site.

Get the latest updates about the carnet de passage, customs, travel advice, health, visas etc. Simply click on the country you want to know more about and start reading. A really good and useful website.

Voodoochile
www.voodoochile.se

Another good website with information on border crossings. The website creator has himself travelled around Africa on his motorcycle and some of the border crossing info is as recent as 2016.

To access this information, go to his website, click the right-hand icon with the motorcycle, select 'Moto and More' at the top and then look for 'Beyond Borders'.

Overland Sphere
www.overlandsphere.com

You will find another good overland forum here.

Horizons Unlimited
www.horizonsunlimited.com

Another great site full of useful information. They also host events where you can meet like-minded people.

The part we used the most was 'The Hubb', which is their forum. It's a really good forum. There are a number of overland forums, but we think this one is the best and the most active. You will find out almost everything you want to know here. If you can't find it, just ask and you will always get a reply.

The Africa Overland Network
www.africa-overland.net

Here you will find information on all previous and current registered overland trips. You can search trips per year, by team name or even by vehicle type. It will give you a list, as well as a little information about the trip and the people involved. You can go to their personal websites and start reading.

It's a good website to find someone with the same car, should you have questions about it. Even for more general matters, it can be very useful to read about others' adventures to prepare yourself for what is to come. You can also list your own trip on this site, if you like.

Expedition Portal
www.expeditionportal.com

A real overland forum with info for 4WD, campers, trailers, motorcycles and even bicycles! Here you will find (brilliant) travelling stories and pictures, equipment reviews, possible routes and a forum.

Wereldwijzer
www.wereldwijzer.nl

This is a forum from the Netherlands, so only for Dutch speakers.

It's not as active as other travel forums, but might come in handy with travellers close by or to source information about administration concerning the Netherlands.

iOverlander
www.iOverlander.com

This isn't a site you will particularly need when preparing for your trip, but you should know that it exists!

iOverlander is a free site created to help travelling overlanders find their next destination. It gathers together a wide range of useful addresses such as campsites, restaurants, petrol stations, etc. It was created by overlanders for overlanders.

You can also help to improve the database by adding your own entries. They now offer you the chance to download data relating to a specific country. They also have a very useful mobile app (more about this later).

Facebook

Facebook is the place to go these days. You can find a group which represents almost anything you can think of.

We used Facebook quite often during our travels. It's a very handy and speedy way of getting information or finding people.

Expats in … (Facebook)

Imagine you need to get something delivered in let's say Uganda, but you don't know anyone there. You might try to find a Facebook group which could help you by typing in 'Expats in Uganda' or 'Belgians in Uganda' (you would use your own country of course, but we're from Belgium) into the search bar. There is a big chance someone in the group will be happy to help you out.

The same applies to finding someone who could give you more specific information. We ended up using the 'Expats' pages quite often.

Overland Sphere

www.facebook.com/groups/OverlandSphere

A Facebook group for overlanders scattered all around the globe. The perfect place to ask any questions you want.

African Overlanders

www.facebook.com/groups/216846841668039

Specific Facebook page dedicated to overlanders in Africa.

Great way to get up-to-date information, as things in Africa change all the time. A lot of members are actually on the road in Africa.

The administrator of this group is Duncan Johnson, owner of the 'African Overlanders' place in Stellenbosch, South Africa. He also makes regular replies on a variety of topics with accurate and useful information.

Overlanding Africa
www.facebook.com/groups/OverlandingAfrica

Another useful page for overlanders travelling through Africa who need to get some info on the road.

Overlanding Association
www.facebook.com/OverlandingAssociation

This is the Facebook page of the Overlanding Association's website.

They regularly post very useful and interesting info here.

Expos
Adventure Overland Show
www.adventureoverlandshow.net

This expo is held in the UK and runs over an entire weekend. Wander around the site, check out display vehicles, talk with overlanders who have recently returned from their travels, look at the exhibitions, etc.

Overland Expo
www.overlandexpo.com

The guys from 'Exploring Overland' also host two expos:

one in Arizona and one in North Carolina.

These are three-day expos packed with information, demonstrations, classes, vendors, etc.

Adventure Northside
www.adventure-northside.com

This event is held in Germany. It's all about overlanding, bush craft, workshops, etc.

Overland Event
www.overlandevent.com

This event is only for motorcycles, but it must be a very good one as you will need to book ahead and it's always sold out!

You can meet other travellers there and hear their stories, see the latest equipment, join in in workshops, drive on off-road trails, etc.

They will even have some motorcycles ready to test drive if you haven't yet decided which one you want. The event is held in England.

Finding the Right Vehicle

This is the hardest part. What kind of vehicle do you want to take? And once you decide on the right one for you, finding it is even harder. You might want to begin looking through the available vehicles and start from there.

Where to Look

Local Sale Pages

You should already be aware of local online selling sites such as Gumtree or specific car sale pages.

Expedition Trucks

www.expedition-trucks.com

These guys specialise in overland trucks and will help you find the right one.

Africa 4x4 Café

www.africa4x4cafe.com

You can also find overland cars for sale here.

The Hubb

www.horizonsunlimited.com/hubb

The Hubb is a forum which connects overlanders all over the globe. You will find loads of information here, as well as a specific 'cars for sale' section.

Facebook Pages

Keep an eye out on the 'African Overlanders' and the 'Overland Sphere' Facebook pages. They post cars for sale on their feed every now and again.

You would find me in front of the computer every morning at 8 a.m. for about a month, searching through the car-sale pages. It took us a while to find the right car, as a lot of the 4x4's on the market are only sold for export. But after an entire month of searching, we finally found our dream car.

—Eef

2

Your Vehicle

If you're planning on becoming an 'overlander', having the right vehicle is of the utmost importance.

We drove through the entire continent of Africa using one vehicle, which means this is the only vehicle type we can review. As we have already mentioned, we left without making any extensive plans and within a relatively short space of time. This meant that a number of things went wrong. We would like to pass on some of our vehicle-related wisdom gained through these experiences, as well as witnessing the struggles of other drivers.

Because we kept the same vehicle throughout our trip, we are unable to advise you as to a make or model. We chose a Toyota because it fell within our price range. Toyotas are also a popular make in Africa, which meant that finding spare parts would be easy (or at least eas*ier*).

Preparing Your Vehicle
Exterior
Bull Bar

Our car already had one. Is it necessary? To be honest, we only used ours as a washing line. Luckily we never had to use it for its correct purpose, which is to hit something without ruining your car. But as you will discover, African roads are packed with people and animals. So, just in case of a cow suddenly leaping in front of your car, you will be happy to have included this piece of equipment on your shopping list.

Whenever you leave your vehicle behind in Africa, you can be sure to come back and find someone leaning on it. They will lean on it as they have a chat with a friend, drink a cup of tea... our vehicle became a magical magnet for all the locals, they just HAD TO lean on it!
—Dries

Snorkel

Handy if you plan on driving through rivers. This is something we never did, but it came with the vehicle we bought.

Roof Rack

A definite must. This is where you will store your equipment.

Extra Lights

We installed two Hella beams on our car, but never used them. You would only really need them if you plan to drive in the bush after dark, and we don't advise anyone to do this when in Africa.

Awning

Useful in both sun and rain! We also used it a lot by placing clothes on it to dry after washing, so we would list this as an absolute must.

Fuel Tank

The amount of fuel you will need depends on the distances you want to cover. We had a tank of 80 litres, plus four 20-litre jerry cans, and never found ourselves without fuel. The only time we needed to use our stock was when driving through Ethiopia and Kenya via Lake Turkana, and even then, we saw somewhere where we could buy fuel at the halfway point. However, there are big advantages to having extra storage on board. The biggest advantage is that you can fill up at places where fuel is cheapest.

We had thought about installing an extra fuel tank but, at the time, this had proven to be too expensive. We had enough roof space for the extra jerry cans, anyway.

Extra Battery

We installed one of these to supply both our fridge and the water pump. It charged while we were driving, and had a switch so that we could turn off the connection when no longer moving, so that it wouldn't drain our main battery. We also had a meter connected, and were therefore able to see how full (or empty) or extra battery was.

Solar Panel

We didn't have one of these, but would definitely take one if we ever did the trip again… not as a necessity, but as a luxury. If you've parked for a few days, the extra battery fizzles out and your fridge will warm up. With a solar panel, you can charge the extra battery even when stationary.

Off-Road

The roads in Africa are not always of the best quality and, as sand shifts easily from under the tyres, off-road gear is important.

- Waffle boards: we used these every time we got stuck. Depending on your budget, you can either buy extremely light roll-up versions or a heavier, non-flexible board.
- Hi-lift jack: we took one with us, but after our first 'stuck in the mud' adventure, we realised we had no hi-lift points, and therefore no place to support the jack under our vehicle. So we ended up using it zero times (and even sold it during our trip). We found we were always able to get out of any situation we found ourselves in without a jack, although the situations might have been solved a little more quickly if we had had the means to use one. So if you plan on taking a hi-lift jack, make sure you

have hi-lift points on your car.

- Off-road kit: a few stretch belts, shackles, gloves … These will all come in handy when another vehicle is there to help you out.
- Spade: great for digging your tyres out of the sand (and when you need to go to the loo in the middle of the desert).

As we were both Africa and car dummies, we had packed a hi-lift jack. However, at our first sticky moment, we discovered we didn't have any hi-lift points … So by our first week in Africa, we already had a lovely hole in the bodywork!
—Dries

Tyres

We chose tyres with extra side protection, which are definitely worth getting, as they will have to go through a lot. You will often find yourself driving over rocks.

We opted for two spare tyres and used both of them.

Before we left, we had read that an extra tyre attached to the outside of the boot as ballast can actually bend the boot door due to the constant vibration. We have no idea if this is true. We had one and never experienced this problem.

Shock Absorbers

Thanks to the state of the roads, you will need strong shock absorbers. On good roads, you won't notice the difference, but when going over potholes and rocks, you will soon find out whether your shock absorbers are sufficiently strong!

Water Tank

We had a 60-litre water tank. As water is scarce in Africa, you tend to use less than you would at home, so we were never without. Our tank had a tap and a pump connected to the extra battery. We met travellers during our trip who didn't have a pump and just stored their water in jerry cans.

Travelling overland in Africa, you often have to make do with the most primitive of basic needs—nothing is straightforward or simple. Cooking is difficult because of the wind, your water needs to be filtered before drinking or you risk becoming ill, vegetables and fruit need to be thoroughly rinsed before eating …

For these reasons, we were very happy to have a pump that allowed us to simply turn the tap on and have immediate and easy access to water, without the struggle of picking the full jerry cans up and tipping them to get the water out—our little bit of luxury during our trip. Sometimes the little things make a big difference.

Filter

We took a water filter made by Katadyn, which was handy for filtering our drinking water. We didn't attach it to the tap as we wanted to use it for as long as possible. We only used it for drinking water and not for cooking, washing, brushing our teeth or any other unnecessary wastage.

Filtering requires both time and effort, but it kept us fit and gave us some lovely upper arm muscle definition. We came across a few travellers who had fitted two separate taps to their water tank—one with filter, one without. We like this idea and will do the same next time.

Fridge

For us, this was an absolute must! We have come across

travellers who didn't use them, but when it's 50°C in the middle of the desert, a stock of cold water is a wonderful thing to have!

We opted for an 18-litre Waeco, which could fit four large bottles standing up and still had enough space for a few other items.

Some people have a drawer fridge, like they often use in lorries. However, because warm air rises, there is less heat loss and therefore less energy usage with top-loading fridges.

Interior

The most important tip we can give here is ... Less is more!

We made a lovely fitted cupboard inside our vehicle, but within the first three months of our trip, we ripped most of it out as it was a) too heavy and b) not practical—even though we thought it was a great idea before we left Belgium! We found it easier to simply keep our possessions in stackable plastic boxes.

On the way, we came across a lot of overlanders and a lot of storage alternatives. Should we do the journey again, we would probably use a different method.

Tips

- During your journey, you will be sampling the local fresh produce. Fresh produce is difficult to keep fresh and mould-free in your vehicle. After the first few months, we realised that fruits and vegetables keep best when stored in a net. This way, there is air movement, even in the warm interior of the vehicle. We fashioned our own net using perforated fabric and used plastic suckers to stick the bag onto the window of our cargo area. This is only useful if your cargo area opens from the side, like so:

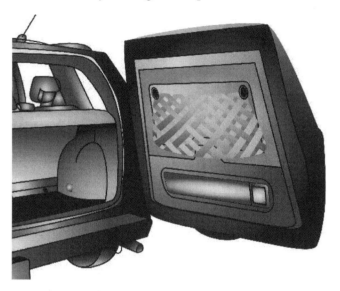

- If your vehicle opens from the side, fitting an extra drop-down table to the inside of the door would be a very useful luxury.
- Use light materials for cupboards, shelves and other 'furniture'. (Google '4WD storage drawers' for ideas).
- Everything needs to be firmly fixed in place, as the roads (if you can call them roads) are bumpy. Everything will have its place, and all drawers and cupboard doors need a good locking mechanism.
- One of the most important things when thinking about storage is that everything you need on a daily basis should be easy to reach. And the things you will be using the most are—no, not clean underwear—cooking utensils.

- There will be a lot of dust during your trip, so dust-proof boxes are a good idea, especially when it comes to your electronic equipment.

Seating

We only had two seats in the front. Should we make this journey again, we might opt for a third seat. Sometimes it's nice to have an extra seat free for people you meet along the way and in some national parks, the rangers are required to join you in your vehicle.

Sleeping Arrangements

In or on the vehicle is the question. Because of space issues, we opted for a rooftop tent.

Read more about this in chapter 10: 'Sleeping'.

Upholstery

Africa is dusty. Any upholstery will quickly get filthy, so an extra cover for your seats is recommended, especially if you have fabric seating. Also remember that leather or plastic seating becomes very hot in the sun, so a cover will protect you from burning yourself!

The sun will also heat the leather or plastic steering wheel, and a fabric cover will prevent burnt hands.

We had some old-fashioned beaded seat covers which were incredibly comfortable and also created a barrier between our sweaty backs and the seating material, meaning we didn't stick to the seats!

Tools

Sooner or later, you will undoubtedly experience a sudden, strange noise emanating from your vehicle and more often than not, this will happen far away from the nearest mechanic. Learning some basic mechanics before you leave is sound advice.

Dries is everything but mechanically minded, so before we left, he took a couple of short lessons with a mechanic. Then, with a tool box and a good quality technical book, we were off!

So what do you need?

- Jack (or hi-lift) and wheel spanner
- Spanners. Make sure you have the right size for every single nut and bolt type used in your car, roof tent, jerry can, etc. Everything needs the correct sized spanner. The roads are bumpy and you will constantly be tightening up nuts and bolts.
- Puncture repair kit = extremely useful!
- Duct tape and plastic ties can solve practically any mechanical problem!
- A good technical manual. We had Max Ellery's 'Toyota Land Cruiser 1990-2002 Diesel Engines Including Turbo: 70's, 80's, and 100's Series: Automobile Repair Manual' from his vehicle repair series and since then, dear Max has become our hero! The book is full of helpful photographs and is written in easily understandable terms, making repairs and disassembling parts as simple as can possibly be.
- Oil. You will always need oil. You never know when you'll have a leak!
- Starter (jumper) cables
- Extra fuses
- African fuel is dirtier than what we're used to in Europe, so you will probably have to

replace your fuel filter at some point. We did this during a major overhaul, which included a complete oil change among other things. You can do this yourself (follow a quick mechanical course at home) or get it done at a local mechanic.

Compressor

On your trip through Africa, you will have to drive on soft sand, which means you will need to let air out of the tyres. To pump them up again, we recommend packing a compressor. It's also useful for blowing clogged dust out of your radiator, camera, laptop, etc.

Tyre Pressure Gauge

A tyre pressure gauge is a worthwhile piece of equipment to have on your trip.

Navigator

Quite useful, we think. We had a Garmin Montana 650 and loved it! It is a very sturdy device, as well as dust- and water proof and it even has a camera.

Maps
Tracks4Africa

We used Tracks4Africa on our navigator and this is an absolute must! This company provides maps of all of Africa, including useful points of interest such as camping sites, petrol stations, water points, shops, mechanics, etc. You can also use it on your computer to plan a route before moving it to the navigator or vice versa.

Paper Maps

Yes, you will probably be using a navigation system, but it's also handy to have paper maps with you. This way, you will have an overview of where you will be driving and it's a lot easier to ask directions or point out an area you want to know more about. Michelin and Tracks4Africa have some good paper maps.

Safety

Tinted Windows

All of our windows (except the front windscreen and passenger windows) were tinted. They keep out the direct sun and so keep the vehicle cooler. However, they also block the view of nosy parkers and prevent acts of opportunistic theft.

Curtain Behind Front Seats

With a curtain, you can further prevent curious eyes from having a peek and decrease the chances of being burgled.

Central Locking

You can be sure that people will try to open the car doors, whether you are driving at the time or not. This is not always done with the wrong intentions. Central locking systems are great; we got into the habit of locking everything the moment we got into the vehicle.

Steering Lock

We also took one of these and mainly used it in northern areas of the continent with low tourist populations. If we left the vehicle for a couple of days when hiking, we would feel more at ease knowing the steering lock was fitted. The further south we travelled, the less we felt we needed it.

Locks

Put locks on everything on the outside of your vehicle that's either loose or can be opened. We put locks around our jerry cans, spare tyres and even the awning zip.

Not that anyone could steal the awning simply by unzipping it, but we did experience someone jumping onto the car and trying to open the zips. He didn't get very far, but there's also the chance you may experience the awning flapping open while you are driving, which we don't recommend.

Two Warning Triangles

Everyone knows what these are for, but it's important to have two. In some countries like Malawi, this is a legal requirement. And you can be sure that when stopped by the police, they will want to make sure that visiting foreigners have both triangles on board.

Fire Extinguisher

Also controlled by the police in some countries. Make sure it has been checked (look for the sticker on the side).

Other travelers had told us that the police had checked their fire extinguishers to see if they have been regularly serviced/checked. Our fire extinguisher check was well overdue, but with a permanent marker this was easily fixed! Of course, you should have a correctly checked and working example on board for your own personal safety, but after all, this is Africa ...
—Eef

Safety Vests x 2

Also controlled in some southern countries.

Extra Reflectors

In Zambia and Zimbabwe, you are required to stick extra reflectors on your bumpers. Whether you have reflectors or not, you MUST have them on the bumpers too. White reflectors at the front, both right and left and red reflectors at the back, right and left.

These are adhesive reflectors that can be bought per metre, and should be cut into a square/rectangle. Should you not have this with you, make sure you buy them in the neighbouring country before entering Zambia or Zimbabwe. You can find them relatively easily.

Extras

Car Straps

Those come in handy in a wide variety of situations: tying something down, quick fix maintenance should you break down ... Take a range of sizes and make sure a very strong one is part of the set—most useful for pulling someone (or yourself) out of the mud or sand when stuck.

ATTENTION!

Never ever use a tow ball for anything else than towing a trailer. Tow balls aren't made to hold the force that is being used when pulling another car out of the sand/mud. The tow ball can snap off and kill someone. (Feel free to Google 'tow ball of death'.)

Also make sure that people aren't standing nearby when pulling another car out with car straps. They can sometimes still break and are dangerous to anyone standing nearby.

Windshield Screen

Not only handy for keeping direct sun out of the vehicle when parked, but also stops others looking in to see what you own, that they would like to own instead.

Rubber Mats

Not mandatory, but they will keep your vehicle a lot cleaner and are quickly and easily shaken out when full of African dust and sand.

Small Bin at the Front

You'll do a lot in the front of the vehicle—eat a biscuit or a banana, wash your hands with a wet wipe—so having a bin at the front is very handy.

Petrol Type Sticker

Stick a sign above your fuel tank cap with 'petrol' or 'diesel' written in various languages. As petrol pump attendants mainly carry out tank filling duties in Africa, it is always better if they know which fuel to use!

Keep It Light

Know how much your vehicle weighs and keep it light!

The lighter the vehicle, the less fuel it will consume and the less deep into the sand or mud you will sink.

Air Conditioning

Our aircon didn't work and we have to admit, it got pretty hot! But thinking back, this wasn't such a bad thing. When you step out from a 22°C car into 40°C heat, it can be a real shock to the system!

Because we didn't have aircon, we left the confines of our vehicle much more often. It wasn't such a sacrifice. Similar temperatures both outside and inside meant we would get out to look at things, or take a time-out to admire the roadside scenery. After all, it was just as hot in the car, so why not get out?

But we did have a small fan that could be plugged into the cigarette lighter. It didn't make the car cooler, but we enjoyed the slight breeze around our heads.

Radiator Seed Net

When on safari and driving through the long grass, a seed net is extremely useful as it prevents grass seeds from clogging up your radiator. However, you can't use it for long, as the radiator will overheat due to the restriction in airflow. We didn't have a seed net with us, but always made sure we blew out the seeds with our compressor after a trip through long grass.

Radio and Lots of Music

An absolute must! African distances are long and no one has enough conversation in them to last the entire journey. Have various types of music with you, because even using the shuffle mode, you'll get sick of hearing the same old songs after a year on the road!

It's best, of course, to take music along using USB or iPod devices. Forget CD's—bumpy roads will destroy them.

Some people also listen to audiobooks. We never tried this, but it sounds like a nice addition.

220V Converter

Very useful for those things you can't charge via USB (laptop, camera battery). In some areas, electricity is a luxury and a converter will make life that much easier. You can buy simple versions that plug into the cigarette lighter, or set something up that will use power from your extra battery.

We had one that fitted into our cigarette lighter, using power from our main battery, which meant we could only use it while driving.

3

Before Take-Off

Time

Take plenty of time to plan, but not so much that you never leave! We were young and impatient and didn't take enough time to prepare for our trip, so we had a few issues on the way. However, this means we can now pass on our many stories to help you either avoid a tricky situation, or change your route to include something amazing we have described.

Test Drive

Take your vehicle out for a weekend (preferably longer) before leaving. This way, you will soon find out what you're missing or what's in the wrong place, etc.

Off-Roading

Take your vehicle off-road and test it out. We definitely recommend this and would even go so far as to say it's a must. If you choose not to then well, it's just another part of the adventure, right?

There are various tracks, clubs and courses which will let

you spend the day off-road and/or have someone teach you useful tips like how to get out of a mud hole and how to get the most out of your 4WD.

Tyre Plugs

On your journey, you *will* get a puncture (we hope you don't, of course), so you'll need to know how to repair one. Find out beforehand how plugs work, because once you're in the middle of the desert, it won't be so easy to consult Google.

You can use plugs when there's a hole in the part of the tyre that is in contact with the ground. Holes in the side of a tyre should *never* be fixed with a plug. In fact, this is extremely dangerous and can cause a blowout.

This is why we recommend tyres with added side protection, as a tyre with a hole in the side can't be repaired and has to be thrown away.

It's possible to fix side holes with a plug. We did this and drove around with one in place for months before being told us how dangerous this was. (Google agreed.)
—Dries

On the Road

Driving in Africa is all part and parcel of the adventure.

It's a long way from what you're probably used to. You will be sharing a rough track with mules, cattle, goats, dogs, chickens, kids, bicycles, scooters and many, many African drivers!

The word 'road' is often an extremely broad description and both your car and your nerves will get rattled. Here are some useful tips to keep you on the 'road'.

Speed

We kept to our personal rule of a maximum of 50 km/h (30 mph) in villages and 70 km/h (45 mph) once out of them, even though the official speed limits were more lenient. We did this simply because you never know what will happen on the road. Animals suddenly jump out in front of you, kids appear from nowhere, potholes pepper nearly every route … you should always be ready to step on the brake.

African roads are a big part of the adventure; kids running across the street, cows sleeping in the middle of the road, mules walking slowly in front of you who completely ignore your honking … The first week, it can be stressful, but then you get used to it and start to enjoy the experience.
—Dries

Accidents

Should you hit someone, no matter how hard you hit them and how strongly your conscience tells you otherwise, carry on driving! Keep going and stop at the first police station you can find.

Why such harsh advice?

In Africa, corruption is rife. If you have friends or money, people can be bought. Police don't offer the kind of service we are used to at home. Locals do not trust them, meaning 'street justice' has developed. People take the law into their own hands. As soon as you stop, the entire village will head your way and not one of them will be interested in your side of the story. You are the foreigner, the rich guy, the outsider, the criminal.

So if you do have an accident—whether you are in the wrong or not—it is dangerous to stop. We've been told this by many, many people, by travellers *and* locals. All travellers—especially white travellers—should always drive on to the next police station, whatever the circumstances.

Safety

A lot of people will tell you that 'Africa is not safe!' before you go, but this is simply not true. It's perfectly safe if you use your wits.

You might experience an atmosphere of tension when travelling in some areas. If you're not sure, call or email your embassy to find out whether there are areas to avoid, or talk to the locals. Locals will know where you are safe to go. Locals will never send you into a dangerous area, as they would like to keep their (few) tourists safe. If we weren't sure about an area, we spoke to several different locals, asking how the situation was at the moment. That way, you avoid any possible 'bad' advice. And, of course, you get to meet the local population and find out more about the country you are visiting.

Maintenance

Morning Check-Up

You will avoid a lot of problems if you take the time each and every morning to do a quick check-up. Make sure everything's where it should be under the bonnet so you will not be taken unawares mid-journey. It goes without saying that water and oil should be a part of every pre-journey check.

Keep an eye out for screws (such as those on a roof tent or roof rack) which, through the constant vibrations and bumpy roads, can work themselves loose.

Window Wipers and Keeping the Windows Clean

We got into the habit of hand cleaning both windows and wipers every morning, as there's a lot of sand and dust in Africa. If you use your wipers for cleaning your windows, they won't last very long. Wipers do a great job when removing water from your window, but can't cope with dust and sand. By keeping them clean and only using them in rain, your window wipers will last 10 months instead of 10 weeks. We are speaking from experience.

Oil Change

You should change the oil every 10,000 km (6,000 miles).

Radiator

Keep an eye on the radiator. Dust, insects and grass can block it. Blow it out every now and again with an air compressor or a high pressure cleaning system.

Air Filter

Blowing out your air filter now and then also doesn't do any harm.

Tyre Pressure

Lower tyre pressure when driving in loose sand. Depending on tyre size and weight, you should lower them from 30 psi to at least 20 psi. When the inner pressure is reduced, the proportion of tyre with direct ground (sand) contact increases, giving your vehicle more grip.

Parking Safely

When leaving your vehicle alone, make sure everything is locked and well covered. Hide everything from view, as some thieves will break the windows for the chance of scoring just a couple of dollars.

Salt

After driving through salt plains or salt water, or even after parking on the beach, you should spray down the undercarriage of the vehicle (with salt-free water!). Salt causes erosion and rust in cars, which you really won't appreciate should something drop off mid-way.

Tyre Rotation

To keep your tyres going for longer, rotate them every 10,000 km (6,000 miles).

It's important to use your reserves in this system. This way, all tyres will wear down at the same rate.

We had two reserves and swapped according to this rotation system:

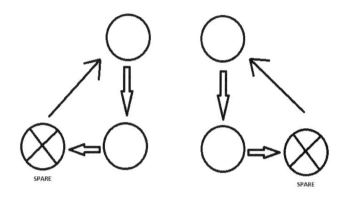

Breakdown

Even though we travellers have to have a warning triangle (or two) in our vehicles, locals do not. If they break down, they lay a small tree or branches in the road. Should you come across branches in the road, slow down and drive carefully.

Police

Be prepared to be stopped by the police on a regular basis. Their main aim will be to try and make money from you: you were driving too fast, you didn't use your indicators, you have your sunglasses on, your vehicle is dirty … They'll always try something. And they don't give up easily.

Take it from us, after the third time you're ready to cause trouble for yourself. However, it doesn't matter how irritating they are, the one rule is this: **REMAIN POLITE AND FRIENDLY!** Be friendly, calm yourself down and don't even think about offering him a bribe. Ninety per cent of the time, the police will have no reason to either stop or fine you. When you keep your cool, they will—eventually—give up. Never forget you're in Africa. The police have a lot of time on their hands. But so do you!

A Few Extra Tips

- Be friendly, patient and calm.
- NEVER give the police any original documents, as it will be difficult to get them back and you will probably have to pay to do so. Give them copies instead. Should they ask for the original, tell them that they are under lock and key in a difficult-to-reach area inside the vehicle.
- Take your sunglasses off when speaking to the police. Not that sunglasses are forbidden, but the police might use it as a reason to fine you. After all, they only need the tiniest reason ... The police also don't think it shows respect if you talk to them while wearing your sunglasses, so just take them off.
- Keep all doors locked at all times, because the police will always want to have a look. Often, they will just open a door without asking for permission. If they insist on looking inside, make sure you are the one opening the door and keep a close eye on what they are doing (and touching).
- You have the right to ask for identification, especially when you have doubts about the authenticity of a particular 'policeman'. We were stopped a couple of times by plain-clothes 'policemen', who flashed a piece of paper that had nothing to do with the police. They'll dream up anything for the chance of free cash!

We've been stopped countless times by police and the funniest (or most annoying) part is that they nearly always stop you for absolutely no reason. They would always ask us for our papers and flick through them while looking at and talking to us (in other words, without actually looking at the papers). A complete waste of time ... but you get used to it.
—Eef

Communication on the Road

Africans use specific signals for communicating with other cars.

- Flashing headlights. When a car keeps flashing its headlights, this means the police are on the road. Should you spot them yourself, return the favour for other drivers.
- Indicators. You'll often come across huge trucks on the road, loaded with gigantic tree trunks, mammoth sewer pipes, bales of straw, cows ... you name it. Unfortunately, these trucks go horribly slow, but in some countries, the drivers are a friendly bunch and will let you know when it is safe to pass and when it is not. The driver will indicate left to let you know when it's safe and right when something's coming the other way. But be careful! In some countries, the opposite applies, so watch what the other cars are doing first upon arrival in the next country.

Time to Stop

We don't recommend night driving for the simple fact

that you are in a strange country, on a strange road with no street lights and where the local population (human and non-human) is nearly invisible. In some countries, it can be considered unsafe to drive at night for more sinister reasons.

Start looking for somewhere to spend the night in good time.

At the start of our travels, we would drive until 4 p.m., then start looking for somewhere to sleep. This gave us two hours to search before it got dark, which was OK, as long as we didn't run into any problems. The worst can always happen; you could end up with a flat tyre, or discover that the camping site you planned to visit no longer exists as the sun sinks deeper and deeper into the horizon ... So start thinking about where you will be sleeping between 2 and 3 in the afternoon, just in case.
Prevention is better than cure!
—Eef

Tanking Up

In Africa, someone normally fills the tank for you, which is really handy! They'll also offer to clean your windows, which is great when they are covered with dust. They do expect a small tip for this. Ask locals or at the campsite what a small tip is.

You should also keep an eye on the cashier and other staff as they all have tricks up their sleeves.

For example, you will ask them to tank up to 30,000 of the local currency. They will fill up to 3,000 and tell you it's done. You might frown and tell them, 'no, I wanted 30,000, not 3,000.' They will go, 'sorry!' and fill it up to 30,000. Which you might think is nothing to write home about (or write in this book about). But you will realise that they have under filled your tank as the counter was already on 2,500 when the man started tanking up (as he didn't reset the counter after the last customer), so he only gives you fuel worth 27,500 and puts 2,500 in his pocket!

This is just one of many scams, so be on full alert!

Off-Road

Tips

- Should you get stuck, it will help if you can make the vehicle lighter by removing spare tyres, full jerry cans, etc.
- If you are using stones and waffle boards, stand far enough away from the vehicle if you aren't the driver. Everything under the tyres will be catapulted out by the spin, which can cause serious damage to anyone standing nearby!

Note

Some of these tips might have you feeling uneasy. We realise this, but please don't let what we are saying put you off from your plans. We are only giving this advice to keep you safe and to let you know what to do when faced with unfamiliar situations. 'Be prepared' is our motto. We travelled through Africa for two years without ever having experienced something dangerous. So enjoy, but be alert. The journey is, after all, half of the adventure.

4

Administration

Car Insurance

We left without arranging car insurance, but there are a few companies that will insure for Africa from home.

In some countries, you are required by law to sign up for local insurance coverage at border control before entering the next country. You will find more information in those chapters relating to specific countries.

Here are a few companies we have been told about by other travellers:

Tour Insure
www.tourinsure.de

The quoted price only includes drivers aged between 25 and 65 years old. Younger drivers (21–24 years old) will have to pay a 25% surcharge. Anyone older than 65 must be in possession of an official medical document stating that they are fit to drive (no surcharge).

Type 1:

- Liability insurance: maximum €500,000 per claim.
- Valid in all African countries; however, some countries require local insurance coverage with much lower payback rates. In this case, Tour Insure will exceed the local policy up to €500,000.

Type 2:

- Liability insurance including full comprehensive and partial comprehensive coverage (a deductible of €2,500 for each claim).
- Only valid for vehicles up to five years old (not motorcycles).

You can find more information on their website and even download an application form. The website is in English and German.

Alessie

www.alessie.com

Offers Third-Party Liability insurance for most of the world, except the country where the vehicle is registered.

Price depends on the period of insurance, make and model of the vehicle and age of the driver(s).

To get a quote you, will need to send an email to alessie@alessie.com. They will forward an application form which you should complete and return along with a scan of your passport and driver's license. They will then consider your application and make an offer.

Campbell Irvine

Although Campbell Irvine used to offer car insurance, they stopped in 2016.

Lockton

Lockton no longer trades in international car insurance.

COMESA (Yellow Card Insurance)

ycmis.comesa.int

The COMESA Yellow Card is a motor vehicle insurance scheme obtained in Africa that is valid in all participating countries. It covers third-party liabilities and medical expenses for the driver of the vehicle and his passengers, should they suffer any bodily injury as a result of an accident to an insured vehicle. It also facilitates cross-border movement of vehicles between COMESA member countries. As this card is valid in many parts of the region, transporters and motorists do not have to buy insurance coverage at each border post they cross.

If you're involved in an accident in one of the participating countries, you are required to report to one of the Yellow Card National Bureaus (this is often an insurance company).

(Info from programmes.comesa.int)

The COMESA is not valid in the country where you buy it, so you must buy local third-party insurance for the country where you purchase the COMESA.

You must buy the COMESA Yellow Card from the same issuing company from which you bought the third-party insurance.

So if you are traveling north to south, you must obtain your COMESA in Ethiopia or Eritrea. If you are travelling south to north, you should obtain your COMESA in Zimbabwe or Zambia, as South Africa doesn't issue the COMESA.

The price of the COMESA depends on various factors: the country where it's purchased, which countries are covered (you can choose which countries you want the COMESA to cover) and the term of insurance.

Countries Where the COMESA is Valid

- Burundi
- Democratic Republic of Congo
- Djibouti
- Eritrea
- Ethiopia
- Kenya
- Malawi
- Rwanda
- Sudan
- Tanzania
- Uganda
- Zambia
- Zimbabwe

Carnet

General Information

The Carnet de Passage en Douane (CPD) allows you to temporarily bring your vehicle into another country and guarantees the country in question that the vehicle will be removed within the time limit stated on the CPD. It this is not done, for example if it is stolen or damaged beyond repair, the various taxes and fees will be paid by the owner.

You need a CPD in the following African countries:

- Egypt
- Kenya
- Lesotho
- Libya
- Malawi
- Namibia
- South Africa
- South Sudan
- Sudan
- Swaziland
- Tanzania

The Carnet de Passage seemed to be a very big deal and a very important document, but at a lot of border crossings, it was as if they had never seen one before; we would have to show them where to sign and stamp.
—Dries

Application

To apply for a carnet, you need to be a member of an automobile association in your country of residence. Google 'Carnet de Passage en Douane + your country' for more information about how to apply.

Guarantee

When applying for the CPD you need to pay a deposit. Should you enter a country and then sell your vehicle, you will not have paid any import tax. The country you are in can then contact the Automobile Association where you made your application and use your deposit to cover the taxes owed.

The amount you pay depends on where you apply. It will be at least 100% of the total worth of your vehicle, and in some countries, this amount can be 150% or even 200% of the total vehicle worth.

Once your vehicle is back in your home country, you need to fill in and return the last page of the carnet, the 'Certificate of Location'. Once this has been done, return the CPD to the Automobile Association and you will get back the deposit.

Joint Guarantee

In some countries, a CPD application will also require a joint guarantor. If you then sell your vehicle during your journey, the country in question can contact your automobile association to cover the import taxes. Should there then be any further debt, the joint guarantor will be required to pay any remaining debts.

Period of Validity

The CPD is valid for one year, but can be extended. If you want to extend the period of validity, contact your automobile association in good time, and apply for an extension. The number of extensions are unlimited.

Cost

A CPD costs US$250–400 and an extension is around US$200.

How It Works

The carnet de passage is an A4 document comprising a number of pages, each page of which needs to be filled in by a separate country. Each page is split into three sections. The bottom (first) section is filled in and removed by border control when you're entering a country. The middle section is filled in and removed when you're leaving the country. And the third (top) section remains in the carnet and has to be filled in, stamped and signed by customs when you're entering and leaving a country.

It is in your best interest to always have the top section filled in, signed and stamped. Some border crossing officials don't seem to have much of an idea about what a carnet is, and you will then have to help them fill it in.

The Southern African Customs Union (SACU) is seen as one country and you only need to have the CPD filled in twice: once when entering and once when leaving. SACU comprises of South Africa, Botswana, Namibia, Lesotho and Swaziland. You may stay in the customs union for a maximum of one year.

Do You Really Need One?

This is a question that we were asked countless times and we have also read about people who travelled without the carnet, but we're not sure how they did it. There will be countries that you cross whose officials have no clue what that little yellow booklet is that you stuff under their noses and you will literally have to point out to them where to sign and where to stamp. But in countries like Egypt and Kenya, they will specifically ask for it. Egypt was the most difficult for us, as our car had had to be shipped in. Shipping out from South Africa also requires a carnet.

Overland Association has a really nice interactive map that shows you in which countries you will need a carnet, where having one is recommended, and where it's not necessary at all.

overlandingassociation.org/carnet-de-passage

Extending Your Carnet

If you travel for longer than one year, you can extend your carnet for another entire year (see under 'Period of Validity'). As you are basically renewing your carnet, you will get a new one sent to you and will therefore either need a postal address or arrange a visit from someone from your home country. We did it the latter and found it very easy to arrange.

However, if you would like to extend your carnet while in South Africa (perhaps you just want to stay a bit longer, or have to wait to get the car shipped out), you can ask for an extension via the AASA (Automobile Association of South Africa). This extension is only valid for a period of 3 months, but cheaper than renewing your carnet for an entire year.

It's a fairly easy procedure. You need to send them:

- A letter stating why the vehicle cannot be exported before the carnet expiry date
- Copy of the carnet holder's passport
- Copy of the carnet counterfoil showing entry into SA

The application will then be forwarded to the South African Revenue Service head office for approval. If approved, they will get back to you with a request for payment.

The current price for an extension is R650.

All of this can be done using email and should be fairly quick; some travellers told us they had got it back within 24 hours. Ours took a week.

Contact details:
Cleodene Sauls
Foreign Travel
Phone: +27 (0)11 799 1009
Email: cleodenes@aasa.co.za

Travel Insurance

Travelling for a year at a time means you will possibly require medical aid at some stage. Your regular health insurance company will often not cover you when abroad. Whether you wish to be insured or not is up to you, but we definitely recommend it.

While you will probably be able to afford local doctor's fees—the price of a visit to an African doctor isn't worth the price you would pay for an insurance package—most world-wide travel insurance companies offer much more than this. For example, should you suddenly become ill or have an accident, some will arrange and pay for your return trip. These insurance companies will also cover your flight home should a close family member die.

Many insurance companies will cover your travels around the entire globe, but most of the packages offered are for four months' coverage.

It took us a while to find an affordable insurance package for longer term, global coverage.

*It was very hard for us to find a travel insurance
that would cover us for long term in Africa, but
we finally found one and were happy to have
one which ticked all the boxes. Unfortunately,
we had a few family members pass away
during our travels and the option to simply call
your insurance company and have everything
arranged for your return home is such a precious
gift during those difficult and emotional times.*
—Eef

Here are some of your options:

Your Credit Card Company

Some credit card companies offer travel insurance with your credit card (Visa, American Express, MasterCard). Give them a call and find out if yours will cover a trip through Africa.

Allianz
www.allianztravelinsurance.com

Provides health insurance for residents of almost all countries, excluding some in America and Asia and most countries in Africa.

Allianz offers 'World Gold Protection', the only insurance package they offer for a trip lasting longer than three months.

Current price: €350 per family per year. So you and your travelling partner(s) will need to have the same address in order to take advantage of this price. If not, you will be paying €285 per person per year.

From the fourth (consecutive) month, there is an additional charge of €40 per month per contract.

VAB

Provides health insurance for Belgian residents.

€105 per family per year (you and your traveling partner(s) must be registered at the same address) or €82 per person per year. From the fourth (consecutive) month, you will need to pay €77 extra per month per contract.

We got our insurance from VAB and were extremely satisfied with the service. Sadly, we had two deaths in the family and VAB flew us back to Belgium both times. Our flights were quickly arranged with a major airline. Taxis to and from the airport were also covered.

All of our medical costs and visits to the doctor when travelling were paid back in the correct manner. We were extremely happy with our decision to use VAB and would not consider travelling without their insurance package.

Tip: If you become a member of Wegwijzer (€30/year), you will receive a 20% discount on your VAB insurance, the equivalent of €160 per family. So definitely worth joining! More info on: www.wegwijzer.be.

Campbell Irvine

www.campbellirvine.com

Provides health insurance for residents from Europe and the UK.

- 12-month worldwide package (not including North America) £463
- 12-month worldwide package (including

North America) £590

It is possible to take out further insurance at the end of the 12-month period if you plan to travel for longer.

Just send an email to info@campbellirvine.com and they will happily send you a pdf with all the information you need.

Clements International
www.clements.com

Provides health insurance for residents of almost every country.

- Insurance starts from around US$360 pp for 12 months, or US$720 for two people for 12 months.
- You may also pay per month (approximately US$30 pp).

For more information and an online quote, go to www.clements.com or contact them at info@clements.com.

True Traveller Insurance
www.truetraveller.com

Provides health insurance for residents of Europe and the UK.

With this company, you can choose between three different insurance types: True Value, Traveller and Traveller Plus (Price range between £180 and £350 pp). The price differences are mainly determined by the amount of coverage you require, for example for medical expenses up to £2.5 million, £5 million or £10 million.

The website is very user-friendly; fill out your details and receive an immediate quote with all the information you need.

World Nomads
www.worldnomads.com

Provides health insurance for residents of almost every country.

They have an easy form on their site that you can fill out for an immediate quote.

Price: Around €900 per person per year

OOM
www.oomverzekeringen.nl

Provides health insurance for residents of the Netherlands. They provide travel insurance worldwide, starting from around €640 pp/year.

You can find all related information on their website as well as request an instant quote.

IMPORTANT!
Before you sign for an insurance package, make sure it covers all the countries you want to travel through, as some travel insurance will exclude countries which have had travel warnings issued against them. This is mainly written in the fine print, so just ask to be sure.

Passport and Visa
Passport
It might seem obvious, but be sure to check the expiration

date on your passport. For the majority of countries, your passport must be valid for at least six months after entry.

Visa

We didn't get any of our visas in Belgium as we didn't plan our trip that far ahead. You can always make timely plans, but in Africa, you never know what will happen on the way. Your car might break down and need parts shipped in from somewhere else, so you will have to wait for the parts and change your plans. And as your visas are on the whole only valid for a few months, they might expire. And when one visa expires, you will have problems with all of the others.

We obtained all our visas on the way, either just before or at the border of each particular country.

You will find more information about visas in the country-specific chapters, but you should also check on forums or with other travellers. Things can change easily and very fast in Africa.

Other Important Documents

International Driving License

Necessary for journeys outside your home continent. Make sure you also have your original driving licence with you, as your international one won't be valid without your regular licence. (We never got checked, though.)

Passport Photos

Bring plenty of these with you, as you will need photos for each visa application and local SIM card.

Copies

Take multiple copies of all your documentation, especially your passport. You will often have to hand in a copy of your passport when applying for visas and buying SIM cards. You should make copies of every document you are carrying and put multiple sets into multiple folders (two should be enough). When police ask for paperwork on the road, you can just hand them a folder. The advantage of this is twofold. Firstly, they don't get to see the originals; African policemen aren't the easiest of characters and sometimes they don't want to give your papers back without you giving them money. This way, if they don't return them, it doesn't matter because you have more copies. Secondly, you will confuse them. There will be many different documents in the folder, so instead of spending time looking at the papers, all they'll do is quickly flick through the lot without bothering to read them before waving you on.

ID tracker

www.idtracker.com.au

The ID tracker is a lightweight wristband that carries a unique ID and PIN, which gives access to the information you chose to provide on their website. The ID and PIN are on the inside of the wristband and can therefore only be seen if the wristband is taken off.

The ID tracker makes sure you can be identified at any time, along with any allergies or medical needs that could save your life.

You're also able to store copies of your passports and travel documents on your profile so you can quickly access them if they get stolen or lost.

Anyone checking your profile using the ID and PIN on your band can activate an emergency email which will automatically be sent to your family members.

One wristband can contain up to five different profiles (five different people).

ID trackers come in a range of styles with prices starting from US$21.95.

5

Health and Hygiene

First Aid Kit

Good health is extremely important, especially when travelling through a foreign continent with diseases very different from those you're used to at home.

You will often find yourself in rural areas, so it's important to have your own mini-pharmacy with you, just in case something happens.

As you will be travelling through malaria territories, don't put off a doctor's visit if you're not feeling well. As soon as we experienced any fever lasting more than one day, we went to see a doctor. We never contracted malaria, but you don't know you have it until it's too late.

It's a disease we don't come into contact with in Europe, which makes it hard to recognise the symptoms.

What We Used the Most

- Painkillers: paracetamol (pain and fever) and ibuprofen (pain, fever and inflammation).

Bear in mind that regular use of anti-inflammatory medication such as ibuprofen can cause stomach ulcers and possible stomach perforation. Should you need to take ibuprofen or other NSAID medication often, have pantoprazole with you to protect your stomach lining and take one on a full stomach with your anti-inflammatory. High amounts of paracetamol can affect the kidneys, so should you experience long-term pain or fever, you should definitely locate doctor.

- Disinfectant (iodine and disinfecting wipes). You will be surprised by how often you will get cut or scratched when repairing the car, getting firewood ... It's important to clean any wound as soon as possible, as you are in a very dusty and warm environment. Dirt will make the wound a breeding ground for bacteria that love the warmth.
- Plasters to cover any open wounds
- Little bottles of saline solution. Ideal for cleaning wounds or flushing out your eyes (the roads are dusty).

Dries isn't much of a handyman; I'm surprised he still has all his fingers! Painkillers and disinfectant are a must must if you're on the road with a (not-so-handy) handyman.
—Eef

Other Important Things We Put in Our First Aid Kit

- Broad spectrum antibiotics: If you go to your

doctor, he/she will probably be happy to prescribe you broad spectrum antibiotics for your trip. If you plan to take doxycycline for malaria prevention, have a word with your doctor as this antibiotic also works against other infections. Remember that antibiotics will also kill healthy gut bacteria, which is why so many people develop diarrhoea when taking them. Together with other causes such as strange food, heat and limited hygiene, a long term bout of diarrhoea can dehydrate you, so be sure to drink plenty of clean water and add salt to your food. Taking broad spectrum antibiotics when your infection is not bacterial but viral will not make you better, but worse, and it is not always easy to distinguish between the two. Don't take antibiotics every time you have a fever and try to get medical advice before using them.

- Something to make you go (laxatives).
- Something to make you stop: we never needed to take anything, but always had anti-diarrhoea medication with us. We didn't even want to think about having a stomach bug in the middle of the desert when you still have to drive three hours to get to the nearest toilet (although sometimes the desert is much more pleasant than the local toilets).
- Medicated eye drops: There is always a lot of dust and sand flying around as you journey through Africa and this can lead to some extremely nasty eye infections
- Antihistamine cream: Eef once came into contact with a processionary caterpillar

(horrible for Eef and horrible for Dries to see). Since then, we always keep some in our first aid kit!

While we were sitting and having dinner, I developed an itch on my neck. I started to scratch; soon the itch had spread to my chest and stomach and it became unbearable. I'd never felt anything like it before, I pulled off my shirt and started scratching like crazy. The itch was driving me insane! I could've just pulled my skin off, it was that horrible. The guards told me that petrol would help, so I covered myself in petrol. It stank like crazy, but didn't help, so I went into the shower. The water on my skin made the itching less uncomfortable, but as soon as I turned the water off it was back. It took ages for the itch to go away, leaving me bright red and full of scratch marks... Now I make sure I'm carrying antihistamine cream with me!
—Eef

Vaccinations

You won't be allowed into some African countries unless you can prove that you have been vaccinated against certain diseases, the most common of these being yellow fever. Some of these countries only require vaccination against yellow fever. However, if you need to get vaccinated, you might as well get other vaccinations or booster shots done which you feel could be important before you leave.

In Africa, you need to be up to date with your vaccinations for the following diseases:

- Hepatitis B
- Diphtheria
- Tetanus
- Measles
- Mumps
- Rubella
- Polio

Booster shots will be required for diseases such as tetanus, diphtheria and measles.

We also recommend the following vaccinations when driving through Africa:

- Hepatitis A
- Meningococcal meningitis
- Rabies
- Typhoid
- Yellow fever

The World Health Organisation has a great interactive map, showing moderate- to high-risk areas for specific diseases.

apps.who.int/ithmap

Malaria

Malaria is a life-threatening disease and common in certain areas all over Africa. We therefore recommend using malaria prevention methods.

Malaria is passed on through mosquito bites. Symptoms usually appear seven or more days after becoming infected with the virus.

These first symptoms are similar to that of the flu: headaches, fever, shivering, sweating, nausea and vomiting. Other symptoms are a dry cough and muscle pain. Such symptoms should always set off alarm bells when travelling in Africa, or shortly after having visited the country. Symptoms tend to present in cycles (and often the symptoms will only present themselves in the evening).

No anti-malaria medication is 100% guaranteed, so if you think you might have contracted the virus, visit a doctor. Malaria is common in Africa, and all doctors and hospitals know how to test you for the disease.

Untreated malaria can be fatal.

You can also buy self-test kits, but without the proper training or knowledge, these can give faulty results. For more information about such tests, go to www.wpro.who.int/malaria/sites/rdt/home.html.

Self-treatment kits exist, designed for emergencies when there is no medical assistance available. These kits are mainly composed of Malarone (Riamet). Get more information from your doctor.

If you feel sick, speak to a doctor IMMEDIATELY. Don't be afraid of African hospitals and clinics—they might be very different to what you are used to and own less equipment than you could ever imagine, but most are hygienic. Malaria CAN be treated and you'll be fine as long as you catch it early. So if faced with any of the above-listed symptoms, don't hesitate. Find the nearest medical services.

Malaria Risk Areas

Below you will find a map and list of malaria risk areas in Africa. During the rainy season, the population of malaria-carrying mosquitos is significantly higher.

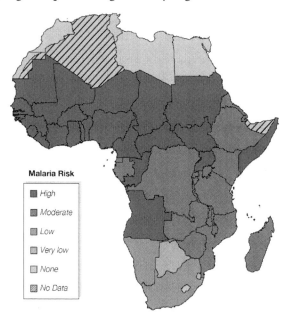

Everywhere

Angola	Ghana	Republic of the Congo
Benin	Guinea	Rwanda
Burkina Faso	Guinea-Bissau	Sao Tome and Principe
Burundi	Ivory Coast	Senegal
Cameroon	Liberia	Sierra Leone
Central African Republic	Madagascar	Somalia
Chad	Malawi	Sudan
Comoros	Mali	Togo
Congo DRC	Mayotte	Uganda
Djibouti	Mozambique	Zambia
Gabon	Niger	Zimbabwe
Gambia	Nigeria	

None

Egypt	Mauritius	Swaziland
Lesotho	Morocco	Tunisia
Libya	Seychelles	

Some Areas

Cape Verde
Limited cases in Sao Tiago Island

Eritrea
All areas at altitudes <2,200 m (7,218 ft.). None in Asmara.

Kenya
Present in all areas (including game parks) at altitudes <2,500 m (8,202 ft.). None in the highly urbanized, central part of the city of Nairobi.

Mauritania
Present in southern provinces, including city of Nouakchott

Namibia
Present in the provinces of Kunene, Ohangwena, Okavango (Kavango), Omaheke, Omusati, Oshana, Oshikoto, and Otjozondjupa and in the Caprivi Strip.

South Africa
Present in the north-eastern KwaZulu-Natal Province as far south as the Tugela River, Limpopo (Northern) Province, and Mpumalanga Province. Present in Kruger National Park.

Tanzania
All areas at altitudes <1,800 m (<5,906 ft.).

Western Sahara
Rare Cases

(Info from: www.cdc.gov/malaria/travelers/country_table/e.html)

Malaria Prevention

No pills will completely protect you against contracting malaria, so whether you take them or not, preparation is the key!

There are two peak times for malaria transmission: just before sunrise (but as most of you will be tucked up in bed, this shouldn't be too much of a problem), and at dusk.

As soon as the sun goes down, the mosquitos appear. So as soon as that sun dips to the horizon, cover yourself and protect any open areas of skin with mosquito repellent. Some mosquitos will bite through thin fabric, so if you're wearing clothes made from thin materials, spray repellent directly onto them.

Mosquito Repellent

The common ingredient in most mosquito repellents is DEET. The higher the concentration of DEET in the repellent, the longer it will protect you. We found that sprays were easier to use than lotions, especially when treating your clothing. Spreading lotion on your clothes isn't that pleasant.

Kite

Kite is a mosquito repellent that is DEET-free. This product targets the mosquitoes' sensing receptors, so apparently, when you spray yourself with Kite, you become 'invisible' to the mosquitos.

At the moment, Kite is working on a patch; a little sticker that you can put on your clothes which will keep the mosquitoes away. At the time of writing, the Kite Patch is not yet on the market, but might be for sale by the time you read this book.

We never used Kite products, but the Kite Patch looks promising. We have therefore decided to include its description in this chapter.

Anti-Malaria Tablets

The three most commonly used tablets are listed below. Discuss the best choice for you with your doctor (where you are going, how long you will be going for ...). Don't forget that these tablets do not guarantee 100% protection and you will need to take other preventive measures when in malaria risk areas.

Try the tablets out before you leave, as they can cause side effects.

Lariam
- Most effective
- Dose: Weekly
- One dose should be taken one week before entering the risk area and for four weeks after leaving the risk area.
- The only malaria tablet that can be taken during pregnancy.

Doxycycline
- Dose: Daily
- Should be taken two days before entering the risk area and for four weeks after leaving the risk area.
- Most common side effects: Nausea in 25% of people taking the drug. Can make skin extra-sensitive to sunburn.

Malarone
- Dose: Daily
- Should be taken one or two days before entering the risk area and for seven days after leaving the risk area.
- Minimal side effects
- Most expensive out of the three options

We travelled through Africa for two years and used doxycycline. We never experienced side effects and it was the cheapest method available. At the start of our trip, we would take one every day and panicked when we forgot to take one. After we had been in Africa for a while, we took them according to where we were. It was therefore important to keep ourselves up to date with the malaria risk of the area or country we were visiting.

As we were in Africa for two years, we thought that taking these tablets on a daily basis would not be the healthiest of options and were quite careful about how often we used them. As soon as the sun went down, we would put on long-sleeved/full-length clothing and would spray areas of exposed skin with DEET.

Bathroom Supplies
Shampoo, Conditioner, Soap and Shaving Foam

Please, please, please use biodegradable ones. There are some gorgeously scented products on the market!

A Few Suppliers:
> www.careplus.eu
> www.ecover.com
> www.sierradawn.com

As we were living so close to nature, we tried to use as little soap products as possible and were surprised at how little soap you actually need to wash your clothes! We had a single bottle of Ecover ecological washing detergent (super concentrated) with us and it lasted us an entire year! (Yes, our clothes were clean). Now we realize just how much soap we waste back at home.
—Eef

Microfiber Towels

Microfiber towels take up minimal space and dry really quickly. We also used them for drying dishes.

Hand Sanitiser

During your trip you will find out what it feels like to be famous—everyone will want to touch you and shake your hand. And some of these hands will be dirty or sticky and you won't always have washing facilities available. A small drop of hand gel will work wonders. Just don't use it in front of anyone, as that's rude.

Nail Brush

Great after a few days in the dust, or after working on the car.

Wet Wipes

A day spent travelling in Africa leaves you dusty and dirty. But a hot bath or shower is not always an option. Wet wipes are the ideal solution. A quick wipe of your face after a dust-ridden journey, freshen your feet before crawling into bed, a quick clean of a knife after lunch in the vehicle… And once we had used a wipe to clean our hands, we reused it for something else like wiping down the inside of the car. Much more eco-friendly!

Sun Cream

Sun cream is simply a must, even when the sun isn't shining. Use it regularly. The African sun is merciless and skin cancer is not just some tall story used to make us buy sunscreen. A little sun and a regular breeze means you don't always feel so hot, but even on days like these, you'll burn a lovely shade of cherry red if you don't use protection.

After-Sun Lotion

You will have to buy this as a punishment for not using your sun cream.

Body Lotion

We got into the habit of using body lotion or after-sun before we got into bed as the sun, heat, dry air and wind can be harsh on your skin.

Make sure you put lotion on body parts that are the most exposed to the elements. In a few years' time, you will be grateful you took the time to look after your skin!

Don't forget to keep an eye on your feet, as you will be in sandals or flip-flops most of the time. When you arrive in Africa from a home country where shoes are the norm, your feet will need time to acclimatise. Your skin will get very dry and can become painfully cracked, so use moisturiser on your feet as often as you can!

Pumice Stone

Callouses and hard skin build up quickly when you run around in sandals and flip-flops. A pumice stone will keep your feet in great condition. (Women tend to use them more).

Vaseline
Heat and wind can cause dry, cracked lips and we found that Vaseline is the best way to keep your lips nice and smooth. Also perfect for cracked heels!

Nail Polish
Travelling through Africa can be described as awesome, but not as comfortable.

As a woman, I paid respect to the different cultures and always wore trousers and long-sleeved shirts, no matter how hot it was.

In Muslim countries, I was ignored, as men aren't supposed to speak to women.

But being a foreigner, you are continuously under scrutiny and you just can't pull off your clothes when they get dirty or sweaty. If you drive through Africa, you will always be dirty, as there is always dust in the car, dust on the car, dust in your hair… Your clothes will fade and stretch due the bleaching effect of both the sun and the constant hand washing.

So, after a few months of traveling I—as a woman—found things pretty tough (especially when tired), until a girl in Kenya offered to give me a manicure and polish! It sounds ridiculous, but wearing nail polish suddenly made me feel female again.

So no, nail polish is definitely not necessary for your travels; you won't die without it. But I still take a bottle of polish along, just for those really tough moments.

Liquid Hand Soap

You will quickly discover that your hands need constant washes. We had a small bottle of (biodegradable) liquid hand soap in the side of our front door. It was a convenient and easy place to keep it. All you need is water ...

Plastic Flip-Flops

These are an absolute MUST in the shower.

Contact Lenses

If you happen to wear contact lenses, bring plenty of fluid, as the fluids I found during our trip were very expensive compared with home prices.

Shower Bag

Sometimes a hot shower is nice (you won't often find one on the road) and one of these thick black plastic shower bags comes in handy.

Just fill up the bag in the morning, put it in on top of your car, and by evening you'll have lovely hot water! (Even placing it inside your car is often more than enough.)

Uribag

The Uribag is a small, portable urinal I ended up using a lot. It's made up of a small lid with a latex bag that can hold up to 1.2 litres. After use, empty and rinse with water and detergent. When you are sleeping in a roof tent in the pitch black with wild animals running around below, the last thing you want to do is climb out of the tent for a pee. So the Uribag is a great piece of kit. I was (and still am) a fan and used it almost daily during our trip! It's also handy for lengthy traffic jams, and can be used sitting, standing or even laying down. And if you are thinking this is a bit out of your comfort zone, you can be assured that your comfort zone will significantly expand during your trip through Africa.

> *I love the Uribag. Personally, I think it is one of the best inventions ever made and I don't know how I would've survived the trip without it. I used it almost every night and once even used it in the middle of a three-hour traffic jam.*
> *—Eef*

The Uribag can be delivered all over the world (prices include delivery).

Female: €23.50/US$25.20/£17
Male: €21/US$23.50/£15.50

More information (English language option) on www. uribag.com

Shewee

The Shewee is a sophisticated, well-moulded piece of plastic that does not leak. Women's toilets are often hard to find in Africa, especially on the road. Sometimes there just aren't enough bushes to cop a squat, and this is when the Shewee becomes a useful piece of equipment. Practise in the toilet or shower at home first. In the beginning, I found it hard to get my head around the fact that I could pee both standing up *and* with my trousers on. (Price £11/€15/US$17)

More information on www.shewee.com

Insect Repellent

This is an absolute must. There are mosquitos in Africa that carry malaria.

The underlying ingredient in most mosquito repellents is DEET. The higher the concentration, the longer the protection.

We found that the sprays were easier to use than the lotion. Some mosquitos can bite through thin material, so you need a spray for your clothes. Spreading lotion on them will just make a mess.

There are other types of insect repellents on the market, such as anti-bug soaps containing ingredients like peppermint and citronella. We never used them, but saw them for sale in the southern parts of Africa.

Other
Apparently, heavily scented toiletries tend to attract more bugs.

Something for the Girls
Menstruating is no fun, and even less so in the kind of hot, sticky, dusty climate you will come across when travelling through Africa. Before we left, I had an IUD inserted as I knew that a) I'd be traveling for a long time (five years) and pregnancy was not an option and b) I forget to take the pill. For me, an IUD was the perfect solution. As the IUD is a hormonal device, my periods stopped completely and I didn't have to worry about finding or taking the pill or finding tampons en route. However, birth control is a personal decision.

But I've still done a bit of research for you girls!

First of all, whichever choice you make, try it out before you go. Hormonal side effects are not pleasant and it's better to be prepared for them or at least have the time to change your method before you leave. Suddenly realising you made a bad choice in the middle of nowhere takes the fun out of travelling.

The Pill

If you've never taken the pill before, or decide to change brand, make sure you test it at least three months before you leave. Everyone reacts differently—it is well known for causing both physical and mental changes.

Your doctor should be able to write you out a year's worth of prescriptions. Take them out of the boxes and they won't take up valuable space.

Menstrual Cups (The DivaCup)

The DivaCup is a reusable, bell-shaped menstrual cup that is worn internally and sits low in the vaginal canal, collecting rather than absorbing your menstrual flow.

Benefits:

- Cost Sparing. The DivaCup, in comparison to other feminine hygiene products, (used for the same purpose) is economically ideal, because it is initially inexpensive and is reusable.
- Eco-friendly. Tampons and sanitary pads are not environmentally friendly and are difficult for the ecosystem to break down. However, with the DivaCup being reusable, it saves the environment from the paper waste that accumulates from use of other non-recyclable hygiene products.
- Safe to wear up to 12 hours. The DivaCup has been thoroughly tested, is strictly silicone-

based and is not made up of anything toxic that may pose health risks. You can wear it safely for up to 12 hours without the hassle of bathroom breaks every two hours.

- Odour Inhibiting. The DivaCup boasts the attribute of capturing odours before they become airborne, so wearing one can help you to contain the unpleasant scents that menstruation can cause.

Downside:

- Difficult insertion at first. Although the DivaCup is made to conform to any woman's body (both sizes pre-baby and post-baby), some users have reported feeling a squishy sensation or like it is going to fall right out. This is a common complaint of using any menstrual cup that will occur when the cup is not inserted correctly. You may also experience leakage when the placement of the cup is not ideal. It may take a few times before you get the hang of inserting it properly all the way up to the cervix, but overall it will become a cinch to use once you learn the trick.

- Manual cleaning of the DivaCup. Another negative attribute to using the DivaCup is the cleaning aspect of it. Since the DivaCup is reusable, one must wash it regularly between uses. The care and washing of the DivaCup may be a deal-breaker for some who are squeamish about stuff like this. But when the overall advantages of sparing harm to the environment, decreasing feminine hygiene expenses, and saving hassle and time are considered, the cleaning part is hardly anything to complain about for most users.

The DivaCup is sold in a few stores around the world (check the store locator on their website to see if one is close to you) or you can buy them online.

Find more info on their website www.divacup.com.

Price: about US$25

Sanitary Napkins and Tampons

All women menstruate, so you will always find some kind of sanitary napkins wherever you are in the world. You will find them even in the tiniest shop, although it might not be the same brand you use at home.

In bigger cities, you will also be able to find tampons, sometimes with the luxury of a variety of brands. If you're worried about not being able to find them, stock up for two periods' worth of tampons or napkins.

Thinx

Thinx are period-proof panties that protect you from leaks and keep you feeling dry.

Really? Yes, really.

They weren't on the market when we were travelling, so I never used them myself, but I've been doing some research and apparently women love them, especially when travelling.

Thinx are knickers made from four layers of material which absorb your period without any leaks and which keep the wearer feeling dry. They come in a few nice styles and look like regular undies. You can wear them all day long, then simply clean them out in cold water and leave them to dry.

I thought this might come in handy while travelling in the middle of nowhere, just to make the unbearable period just that little bit more bearable.

Let us know how what you thought of them.

Price: US$24–US$38

www.shethinx.com

General Health
Water
Drink plenty of water! It's hot—very hot—and you will sweat a lot and lose fluids all day long.

> *We cannot stress enough how important it is to drink a LOT of water, as the temperature in some areas is excruciating! We filtered our water. This removes bacteria, but unfortunately not the smell or the colour; be prepared to drink a variety of shades of green!*
> *—Dries*

In the morning, we always made sure we drank at least two cups of tea, to start off our day with a good fluid intake; many people don't like to drink too much in the morning.

You will probably also meet foreign cyclists on your travels, who—for some absolutely crazy reason—have decided to cycle through Africa. Be nice and give them some fresh water, as they can only carry so much on their bike. In the beginning, whenever we saw a cyclist we would simply wave enthusiastically or even stop to have a little chat. It was only after our third cyclist on a very, very, hot day, and as we were drinking some lovely, fresh, cold water, that we thought, 'shit, we should have offered that poor cyclist something to drink!'

Cuts and Scratches

It's important to clean a wound as soon as possible as you will be driving in a very dusty and warm environment. Dirt will get deep into the wound, while bacteria grow best in the heat.

Under the Weather?

Not feeling right? A slight fever? Not sure what is going on?

Get it checked out!

You're in a strange country with strange diseases, so don't take unnecessary risks. Although clinics in Africa will look badly equipped compared to clinics back home, there are skilled doctors completely willing to help you and able to recognise symptoms you don't have the knowledge to recognise.

Dental Check

Get a full dental check before you leave—you don't want to end up in the middle of nowhere with toothache!

6

Money

'You've been travelling for longer than a year? Wow, you must have rich parents!'

No! People can't be that rude! You think?

They are! This is just one of the comments made to our faces, mainly paired with a look of suspicion: 'Either the parents are rich, or she's a prostitute and he has sold a kidney'.

And we've have even seen that look on our friends' faces.

When you don't have a job and are young (!), people just don't seem to believe it is possible to survive.

But as I write this, we've been travelling for three and a half years. And we have survived.

On the road, you quickly learn the value of money (or the lack thereof). You learn to survive on so much less than you would 'need' back home. The importance of money quickly fades into the background when you're travelling ... OK, that last one's a lie. But when you're travelling, money isn't the priority anymore; you learn to make do with less. You might even be happier that way!

We're not going to give you a budget in this book, nor are we going to tell you how much we've spent (we don't want to be reminded about the amount of money we've spent on fuel alone!). There are quite a few travellers who list their outgoings and budgets on their websites.

We are also not the ideal people to give advice about budgets; we were young and left without any budget whatsoever. We would travel until we ran out of money and then find work. The longer we were away, the better we got at managing our budget. That way, we never completely ran out of money again.

In this chapter, we would like give you some tips about how to save money on the road, how to make a little extra on the side and so on.

Nothing major, no million euro money laundering tips, but some of them might help your pounds, euros or bartering beads go just that little bit further.

Before You Leave
Bank Cards

Before you leave, make sure that you can use your cards worldwide. A Visa card is essential for withdrawing money in some countries. It's a good idea to sign up with two different banks (with two different bank cards). That way, should something go wrong with one bank, you still have another account to use as a backup. On one occasion, one of our bank cards couldn't be used and, with it being a Sunday, we couldn't contact our bank. Luckily we had another card to fall back on, which allowed us to withdraw cash that day.

American Dollars

The American dollar is the number-one choice of currency in most African countries. In some countries, you can only pay for your visa with USD, so make sure you always have some in hand. You can exchange USD everywhere in Africa for local currency.

We didn't have any dollars in Sudan, and needed a visa to cross the border into Ethiopia. Although we had Sudanese pounds, Ethiopian birr and euros with us, they would only accept American dollars.

Should you visit Zimbabwe, bear in mind they don't have their own currency and only use USD. Because of this, no new notes are printed and the circulating notes have been in every fisherman's pocket and every market woman's cleavage at some time or another. So, it's always nice to have some fresh, clean American one-dollar bills with you.

Of course—dummies that we were—we didn't have any USD, but luckily there are a lot of nice people in the world! The first time we were helped out by a local Sudanese man—and even today, we're still in contact. After that, whenever we met travellers from America, we would ask if they had some spare USD.
So we never ran out of USD again.
—Dries

On the Road

We didn't have a safe to keep our cash, passports and valuables in, as we thought that if anyone got into our car, that would be the first thing to go and we would lose everything in one fell swoop. We split up our money in a few socks, hidden amongst our clean socks. No one would bother to look there.

Sponsoring

You will soon realise that preparing for a trip like this requires a lot of money. An extra light, a new box, a spare tyre, a back-up charger… the list never ends.

Eef decided to try her luck with a few businesses one morning, asking for sponsorship in exchange for adding their logos to our website. We didn't think we'd get anywhere, as they probably had plenty of sponsorship deals. Surprisingly, most of our requests were accepted. So, ask around. You have nothing to lose!

Rent Out Your House

If you have your own house, why not rent it out while you're travelling? This way, it pays for its own expenses; insurance, mortgage, taxes …

If you're lucky, you might even make enough to cover an additional, if small, monthly income.

Sell, Sell, Sell

If you go travelling for a long period, you just can't put everything in boxes.

We sold a LOT of our stuff, both the things we didn't need any more and the things we could buy again once we got back.

I also sold a lot of my clothes, which I was sure I wouldn't be wearing once I got back; we left when I was 25 and I will be 30 when we get back, and I'm sure I won't be looking for my old miniskirts or the pyjamas with the big frog on it the moment I step into the front door.

On the Road

How Much

Before you go to the market, find out from someone (local) how much you should pay for whatever it is you want to buy. If you can't find out before you go to the market, ask the price in a few different shops before you buy. The first one will say 100, the second one 30 and the third one 35; foreigner prices are often just 'spur-of-the-moment' prices, and some shopkeepers think slower than others.

Haggling

Part of the shopping adventure is haggling! It's not rude, it's how African culture works; everyone bargains, even the locals. As you are a foreigner, they will raise their starting prices a lot more than they would for their local customers. Another reason to find out how much you should pay for a specific item.

We were always fine about paying a bit more than the locals, as we're foreigners—tourists—and tourists are a source of money. But we would never agree to pay prices ten times higher than those offered to the locals. We got very good at haggling.

Prices will seem cheap at first, as you will be comparing them with home, so it's easy to give in to the first offer. However, while it might still be cheap for you, the shopkeeper might be making a 1000% profit.

By paying the asking price, you are encouraging sky high prices for foreigners. Which means you will make life that little bit more difficult for future travellers, and for yourself.

Your money will run out much more quickly.

What is great about knowing the correct price beforehand is the realisation of how many people are actually very honest when it comes to the asking price. And, of course, you won't insult the honest shopkeeper by making an absurdly low offer.

In the beginning, haggling was a very alien experience to us. But it's simply expected of you. Now, Dries is the haggling king!
—Eef

Barter

Something we love about Africa is the swap mentality, the ability to buy something with something you don't want or use anymore. This is common practice, especially in rural areas, as here the locals will often be happier with a T-shirt or food than with money. If you give cash, they might have to walk miles to the shop to exchange that money for food.

Often you can pay for something using a combination of cash and barter goods.

Money, Money Everywhere

During your African travels, you will be seen as a walking wallet—people will just see dollar signs bobbing along. They will think you are rich—very rich—and that you will be happy to pay them for the slightest service.

If you ask someone for directions, they will more than happily show you the way. Then, as soon as you're there, they will hold out their hand. Even if it was only a ten-metre walk. So ask them to tell you the way instead of show it. If they insist bringing you there, tell them that you won't pay them and make this very clear as they will still try to get you to pay up in the end.

Of course, there are many good-hearted people. But sad to say, the majority of the locals you encounter will want money for whatever they 'offer' to do for you.

Exchange

Always look up the exchange rate before you enter a new country. If you've no clue, the exchange offices will rip you off big time!

At some border posts, you have to pay third-party insurance or something else in the local currency, so you have to exchange currency.

We always tried to exchange our leftover money with other travellers—this way no one has leftover money. Travellers' rates are fairer, too.

Bribes

Bribery is common in Africa, but we would advise you not to do this. Once it gets to be a habit, road trips through Africa will become more expensive than a five-star tour of Europe.

The only thing you need is patience; locals will always try to get more money (a bribe) out of you. Just refuse to take a hint and take your time. You're in Africa. Time is not an issue. After a while, they will give up.

During our trip, we paid one bribe, and still feel bad about it. We had just spent four hours at the Kenya/Uganda border with a very difficult customs officer, so when we finally drove into Uganda, we were completely exhausted and just wanted to get to the nearest campsite as soon as possible. 500 metres into the country, we got pulled over by the police (naturally). According to the police, we had done something wrong (naturally) and had to pay a fine. We talked him down to a third of the price, paid it and drove on. I think we were just too tired to think clearly. But just five minutes later, we suddenly thought, 'What did we just do? We bribed him!' We've never paid one since ...
—Dries

Tips

Always look up how much you should tip if you go to a restaurant or bar. This isn't just so that the foreigners aren't charged crazy prices, but bartenders and waiting staff are paid via tips. Refusing to tip would be wrong.

We knew nothing about the tipping culture and had hardly

tipped at all. After finding out about how the hospitality staff depends on tips, we felt incredibly guilty. We won't make the same mistake again!

The further south you go, the more you will see security staff at big supermarkets, or gas station attendants. Find out how much you should give them. It's nearly always a tiny amount.

ATMs

In the big cities, you are likely to find ATMs. Withdraw money when you find one, as you will need cash on a daily basis. Most markets and shops don't work with credit cards.

As withdrawing money in a foreign country costs money (exchange rate + withdrawal fee), we always withdrew the maximum amount allowed and hid it in smaller amounts in our vehicle.

Working on the Road

We left in a rush, too young and too impatient, so when we ran out of money within the first few months, it wasn't much of a surprise.

And if we could turn back time?

We might have taken more time to prepare, saved a bit more money, worked a bit longer and calculated our expenses a bit more realistically ...

But if we would have worked a little longer, saved a little more, calculated our expenses a little bit more realistically, we probably never would have left!

So, when you ask us if we, in hindsight, would have done anything differently? Nope. Nada. Neen. It was all part of the adventure, part of the challenge, part of the 'how solid is your relationship?' test. Hopefully you have been working, saving and calculating much better than we ever did, but should you need some tips about 'working on the road', here are a few:

Working in Africa

We can't tell you too much about this, as we only tried looking for work in two countries, but it's always good to know.

We had originally planned to work in Kenya, but getting a work permit proved to be difficult, so we tried in the next country ...

... And Uganda said yes!

You can get a three-month work permit here quite easily and cheaply. Your employers will arrange this for you, and it costs approximately US$200 (US$100 for the permit, and US$100 for the fixer). If you want to know more, we advise you to ask questions on Facebook pages such as 'Expats in Uganda' or 'Expats in Kampala'.

If you don't want to stay in one place while working, there are other ways of earning money while travelling.

We spent seven months working in Uganda. It was, for want of a better word, an experience. You get such a close look into Ugandan life: the people, the work ethics, the corruption. The experience was fun, special and completely unique. We've done it. But I don't think we will do it again. —Dries

Calendar

Make a calendar using some of the best photos of your trip.

Whatever you make out of this enterprise, you can either use or donate to the charity of your choice, or a bit of both.

After researching a few companies, we chose Vistaprint to print our calendars. We created them online, sent a test copy home, made any necessary changes, and then had 50 printed!

We sold them through our website, but the printed calendars were sent to Belgium and family members helped to post them to the right person. So you will need a helping hand at home.

Postcards

Make postcards of your best pics and sell them online.

We found a few websites, compared them and chose Zazzle (www.zazzle.com).

What's great about Zazzle is that you have your own page on their website, and can pass on the web address to friends, family and acquaintances. They are taken straight to the seller's website and can easily place an order, and every couple of months, the seller receives a payment.

Upwork

Upwork is a freelancing website, where you can find all kinds of jobs … translation, article writing, blog writing, data collection, graphics, IT, website design …

We worked via Upwork for a while and earned quite a tidy sum.

It takes a while to get started, as without positive reviews, you have to charge next to nothing in order to be offered work. However, once you have a few good reviews, you can charge more. And the more positive reviews you get, the more you can increase your fee.

You won't get rich and, if you live in Europe, you might not earn enough to make a living, but in Africa, the money we earned went much, much further!

Eventually we ended up earning more on Upwork than we did in our jobs in Uganda.

Write Articles

Email a few 4WD or travel magazines in your own country, or even one in a country you are travelling through. Many of them would love to print your adventures. Apart from the fact that you will earn money, it's also nice to let your family and friends know that your stories will be published.

7

Food

Cooking on the Road

On the road, cooking is a totally new experience. You are completely dependent on your clean water supply, local produce and the wind. You will have to learn new cooking techniques, get used to new tastes and familiarise yourself with strange ingredients. Going shopping or eating at a restaurant in Africa will open your eyes to a new culinary world.

Your Kitchen

Your kitchen will be much more primitive than back at home, but this doesn't have to mean it's less fun.

Burner Stove

We chose a two-burner Coleman for the simple reason that it worked on liquid fuel or unleaded gasoline, which we could find everywhere. Even though it did its job, we weren't 100% happy, as we found it hard to get a blue flame (even though we followed the instructions). It's quite messy to use when filling up with fuel, which can make it pretty dangerous when lighting it. But we did come across travellers who loved it, and wouldn't part with it for anything. So maybe ours was faulty, or maybe we were just a bit clumsy! Should you go for a fuel stove, carrying around 20 litres of fuel is unnecessary as you don't use much. We started off with a 20 litre jerry can, but transferred some into two empty water bottles and gave the rest away. Less weight and more space! Please note: they say it's not safe to store fuel in plastic, but we did without any problems whatsoever. The choice is yours.

We also thought about bringing a gas fire, but had read that gas bottles can explode in the heat and with so many potholes in the roads didn't think this was a good idea. But again, we came across lots of travellers who used them without any problems. The only negative thing about gas is that the nozzle fitting can be different from country to country, so you need a selection at hand so that you are always able to fill the tank.

We were once high above sea level in Ethiopia. It was freezing cold and extremely windy. Luckily, there was a little hut that we could use, and we decided to use the Coleman burner inside (even though it was only recommended for outside use). How right they were! Somehow fuel had leaked from the burner and it caught fire. Luckily, only the fuel burned and not the table. Unfortunately, the burner didn't survive my Olympic-rated long-distance throw outside.
—Dries

Foldable Equipment
Nowadays nearly everything can be folded, so that it takes up less room. Foldable bowls, colanders, even kettles come

with foldable parts!

Our best buy was a foldable wash basin with handles. It didn't take up much room, and was really strong. A word of advice… be careful of sharp knives! Ours was covered with duct tape and puncture kit tape to cover up the holes!

Tea Towels
We used small microfiber hand towels for drying up, because they didn't take long to dry out again.

Plastic/Aluminium/Metal
We don't need to tell you that plastic, aluminium and metal don't break as easily as glass and stone, and also weigh less. Be aware that aluminium and other metals will get incredibly hot when you put something hot in them.

Pots and Pans
Pots and pans with removable handles will also need less space to store.

Extras
Even if you are only travelling in a group of two, always take at least one extra everything. You can lose or forget something on the road, and it's great to have a reserve. But most of all it's great to be able to invite someone else to a meal.

A lot of camping sites have security guards who have to stand outside in all kinds of weather because you are there. Offering a cup of tea in your extra cup is always much appreciated!

Kelly Kettle
Again, one of our 'can't do without', and we were so glad to have her with us.

With a few twigs, you will get boiling water in no time. No electricity. No gas. Just a few twigs—you'll find them everywhere, and they are free!

The Kelly Kettle is a hollow kettle without a bottom, and with a double wall which holds the water. Because the water is kept in a narrow channel between the double walls, the water reaches boiling point incredibly fast!

You can buy one in various sizes. Prices are around the £50 mark.

More info: www.kellykettle.com

Water
We had a Katadyn filter that we used to obtain drinking water and were very happy with it. Read more about the filter in Chapter 2: Your Vehicle.

Rubbish
Read more about this in Chapter 7: One With Nature.

Coffee
If you love your coffee, there is a little machine called 'Handpresso' which (apparently) makes lovely espresso. You only need hot water, ground coffee (or one of their pads) and your own two hands. We didn't have one with us, but we heard a lot of positive things about it.

Price: €65–€150

More info: www.handpresso.com

Eating on the Road
You will be ultra-dependent on local produce during your trip, and will quickly realise how spoiled we are back at

home. At home, we can find everything we need, whether out of season or not. Fresh strawberries in winter? Why not?!

In Africa, you will quickly discover in which seasons fruit and vegetables are ready for harvesting.

Tomatoes are not perfectly round, and bananas are not canary yellow. Your meals will therefore look different, and you will come across things you have never seen or tasted before. But isn't that one of the reasons you are planning this trip?

Local Markets

You will do the majority of your shopping here, and it takes some getting used to. You need to learn how to find what you want and then haggle over the price. But you will quickly get the hang of it and will probably end up enjoying the experience.

When buying at a local market, you are helping the locals, so keep this in mind when you suddenly come across a supermarket.

We ate bananas for two months. Nothing but bananas. Bananas, bananas, bananas. I paid €5 for an apple when I found one!
—Eef

Supermarkets

The first real supermarket we found, where everything had a price, and everything cost more, was in Nairobi, Kenya (when travelling south, of course!).

Water

Try not to drink tap water, and definitely don't at the start of your journey. Your body will not be ready for the shock and—especially when travelling north to south—tap water is not drinkable.

Filter or boil water before drinking it.

The further south you go, the more the countries cater to tourists and the more the tap water is treated and drinkable.

Always order drinks without ice, as ice cubes are nearly always made from tap water.

Only drink hot tea or coffee. If it is lukewarm, the water may not have been thoroughly boiled and will not have been filtered or purified in any way.

> *If you drink fresh fruit juice, be sure it has not been diluted with water! On our first day in the Sudan, Eef had one and didn't come out of the loo for the next four days.*
> *—Dries*

Meat

Never eat raw meat!

In Ethiopia, raw meat is a delicacy, but we strongly advise you not to try it.

You will probably buy meat at the local market and it's not beautifully packed as it is at home. It hangs out in the open, in the heat, and is often covered with flies. So cook it well.

And don't worry too much. Back home, health laws mean we panic if meat hasn't been chilled for two hours and we throw it in the bin! We never got ill from eating cooked meat in Africa.

Raw Fruits and Vegetables
Wash fruit and veg thoroughly, but not with tap water! As you won't always have enough filtered water, peeling is sometimes the better option.

Ice Cream
Even on the hottest days, don't buy ice cream from street vendors or small supermarkets.

The electricity supply in many countries is unreliable, so ice cream will melt, then freeze, then melt again, and freeze again. This means your lovely, cold ice cream (and many other dairy products) could be swarming with bacteria!

Also, the local ice lollies are made with tap water, so they should also be a no go!

Secret Stash
When travelling, you will find that you miss some of the tastes of home. Take a few items with you that will keep well in the heat and hide them in a secret place ready for emergencies.

Go on, treat yourself!

Local Delicacies
Try these out! They're often cheap and delicious!

Just don't buy ready-to-eat fresh vegetable dishes, as the vegetables probably haven't been washed and you have no idea how long those chopped tomatoes have been sitting in that bowl.

In some countries, eating out is cheaper than cooking a meal yourself (especially as you will often be charged more at the market because you are a foreigner).

Invitations

In a lot of rural areas, you will be invited into people's homes for African tea and local biscuits. If you walk around in villages around lunch or dinner time, you will probably be invited in for a meal. It's rude to decline such invitations, so if you don't want to eat in someone's house, don't walk around in villages around mealtimes.

Experiment

You will have fewer ingredients available and will therefore have to experiment at meal times.

Some of the things we did:

- Sausages: either eat them as sausages, or cut them open and use the mince for pasta sauce or added to rice. Really tasty!
- Couscous burgers: as cooking is so much more complicated; you will often make one-pot meals. Mix mince with couscous (and an onion if you have one) and make burgers. Add your sliced vegetables and it's ready to eat.

Citrus Fruit

Elephants love citrus! Or at least that's what we heard. Should you get to camp in a national reserve or at the edge of elephant country, make sure you put all your citrus fruit into an airtight box (preferably in the fridge). We've heard stories of elephants breaking windows to get to an orange. There was also an elephant that pulled the roof tent from a car, because the people had left an orange peel in the bed. So hide them well!

8

At One With Nature

There is no recycling in Africa, nothing like we are used to at home. Spray cans are simply thrown into the bush or end up on the local garbage dump. The problem here is that people—and often children—will go through your rubbish. Besides the fact that spray cans are bad for nature, imagine that a child gets hold of it, pierces it, and throws it into a fire. And not only could your spray can be dangerous for kids and nature, in your vehicle it can get hot—and we all know that gas cans and heat do not mix. Ditch pressurised cans. We used roll-on deodorant. They may be messier, but are much safer for the environment and your vehicle.

During your journey, you will be living close to nature; almost all the water you use (showering, washing dishes, washing the car) goes directly back to Mother Nature. Water is not filtered and reused in many parts of Africa. We find it important to care for our planet as best as we can, so we used biodegradable soaps whenever possible. Nowadays, you can find all kind of eco-soaps (shampoo, shower gel, shaving cream, dish washing soap, laundry detergent) in all kinds of shapes and scents. Some available products:

www.careplus.eu
www.ecover.com
www.sierradawn.com

But beware, just because the soap is biodegradable doesn't mean that it is good for nature, so use as little as possible. You can wash your clothes with much less soap than they recommend on the back of the bottle!

Waste

In Africa, there is no recycling organized by the governments and there are some countries that don't seem to have heard of rubbish bins; everything goes straight onto the street.

Waste remains where it is dumped, polluting the soil; animals eat bits of stale food together with the plastic wrapping; children open bags containing broken glass and leaky batteries; the winds blow our bin bags across the countryside—where they end up, we'll never know. But there's no-one around to collect our rubbish and dump it in the appropriate site.

Waste policies in Africa are useless. As travellers, it is important that we produce as little waste as possible. Here are a few tips:

Reuse

The wet tissue you just used to wipe your face clean is still handy to wipe all the dust from the dashboard or get those annoying bird droppings off the windscreen.

Give Away

Did you eat anything from a can? Wash the can out and put it somewhere along the side of the road (mainly in the northern African countries. You wouldn't do this in Cape

Town, for example). Families use empty cans to fetch water, cook, etc.

The same goes for a stretched or faded T-shirt you no longer wear, or an empty plastic box and so on.

You will be amazed at what they will recycle in Africa.

Reusable Bags

In Africa, they are big fans of plastic bags. In supermarkets, they will pack your purchases in as many plastic bags as is humanly possible: meat in one, detergents in another, vegetables in another. Be kind to the environment and bring your own reusable bags to the store.

Burning

Although this is not ideal for the environment, it's better to burn your waste than to have it affect local wildlife or pollute the water sources.

Make sure your fire is definitely out before you continue on your way.

Never bury your waste: not only does it contaminate the soil, rubbish can also be dug up by wild (and domestic) animals which could be injured or poisoned.

In the beginning, we collected all our rubbish in a bag and asked someone where we could leave it. They were very friendly and took the bag from us with a warm smile, walked across the road, and dumped it in the gutter.
—Dries

Decomposition Time

This is the amount of time various items need to decompose in the open air, under the influence of rain, sun, insects and fungi (it takes even longer when buried).

- Paper: two to four weeks
- Vegetables and fruit scraps: two weeks to six months
- Plastic bags: ten to twenty years (up to 500 years when buried underground)
- Aluminium cans: 100–500 years
- Plastic and glass bottles: 500–1,000,000 years
- Polystyrene: never

Human Waste Disposal

Use toilets where provided and never flush anything other than toilet paper.

You will often be in a situation where there aren't any toilets around (when you're camping in the desert, for example). If you find yourself in a toilet-less situation, dig a small hole around 15 cm deep and cover it afterwards with soil and a rock. Don't bury your toilet paper—carry it with you or burn it on the spot. Make sure you're at least 100 m from any water source.

Washing

Most of Africa is without a wastewater treatment programme.

- Don't use detergents or toothpaste in or near a water source, even if they are biodegradable.
- Make sure you're at least 50 m away from a water source.
- If you're washing in a water container, disperse

the waste water widely over the ground instead of in one spot. The bigger the area you cover, the more soil there is to absorb your waste water, and it can penetrate less deeply into the ground.

Water

Conserve water! This speaks for itself. Water is like gold in Africa, so try to minimise your water use.

You will quickly discover how little water you actually need; at home you might brush your teeth with the tap open, but in Africa you can use half a cup and realise that even that's more than enough. Take these habits home with you!

Plastic Bottles

When travelling for longer periods of time, it is both ecologically and financially sounder to use a water filter. Africa is hot (sometimes incredibly hot) and you need to drink a lot. Buying water can become costly in the long run and that's not even considering the mountain of plastic you are producing as you travel!

Remember that Africa doesn't recycle and rubbish is just tossed out of the window and into the road, where it is swept along by the wind and mainly ends up in water holes.

So we advise not to buy water in plastic bottles, but to carry a water filter.

Hotel Stays

Even if you end up staying in a hotel, you can also contribute to the environment.

- Reuse your hotel towels and bed linens in the hotel to conserve water.
- Limit energy use by turning off your lights and air conditioning when you leave and unplug battery chargers, even if they're not charging anything.

Souvenirs

In Africa, you will find the most beautiful and strange souvenirs. You might come across souvenirs made from animal parts such as coral, tortoiseshell, ivory ... Such souvenirs might be illegal, so be mindful of what you buy.

Recycle Before You Go

You might have new items in your vehicle still in their original wrapping (a spare cable, new toothbrush). Unwrap them before you leave and recycle while you still have the opportunity.

Unsubscribe

When living at home, you will probably have a newspaper subscription, get your bank statements by post, receive advertising from your favourite shops, etc. So be sure to unsubscribe from all paper mail before you go—and save trees.

Eat and Drink Local

Try to avoid products that are imported; this way you will reduce your carbon footprint (as goods have to be transported by air, road or rail). Besides saving the environment, you will also get to taste some new things.

Batteries

You probably will have items with you that work using batteries—torches, cameras, etc. Use rechargeable batteries. As we've said before, Africa does not have recycling plants and batteries are VERY harmful to the environment.

Driving Green

Driving green not only helps the environment, but will also save you money. You might think that the following tips won't make much of a difference, but remember that you're going to drive across Africa—after 30,000 km (19,000 miles), it all adds up.

Getting Around

Of course, you're travelling by 4WD and you need it to get from north to south or vice versa, but if you're staying at a campsite, walk to the local market by foot or take a bicycle-taxi to the museum. It's good for the environment and your personal fitness levels, and you will be supporting local businesses at the same time.

Use one of the local taxis/buses instead of your own private taxi. Take it from us, it's an adventure you will never forget.

Pack Light

You will (and have to) leave home with a lot of stuff, but remember, the lighter you pack, the less fuel you use, the more money you save and the less damage you do to the environment.

The EPA (Environmental Protection Agency) estimates that for every extra 100 pounds (45 kg) your car carries, it loses two per cent in fuel economy. (Source: auto.howstuffworks. com)

Tyre Pressure

Make sure your tyres are properly inflated—if your tyres are underinflated, your car will use more fuel.

Air Conditioning

Air conditioning increases fuel consumption, so don't use it when you don't need it.

We didn't have air conditioning in our car (well we did, but it didn't work) and yes, sometimes it was really hot! But because we didn't have an aircon system, I think this made us less reluctant to leave our car and take a look at what was going on outside. After all, it was hot both inside or outside the vehicle.
—Eef

Driving Style

One of the best ways to improve your fuel economy is to change the way you drive. Speeding, accelerating and braking hard can deplete efficiency by 33 per cent, according to the EPA (Environmental Protection Agency) (Source: fueleconomy.gov).

When you're approaching a stop light and you see it's turning red, start to slow down instead of stopping at the last minute. This is one of the easiest ways to save fuel.

Higher gears are more efficient, so go a gear up as soon as possible.

Charging

Charging your gear through your cigarette lighter is easy while driving, but the engine has to work harder when charging and so increases fuel consumption. Think about purchasing a solar panel.

9

In the Wild

Camping

In a lot of countries through Africa, you're allowed to camp in the wild and it is amazing. Driving off-road and putting up your camp in the middle of the desert ... the feeling of being 'the only person in the world' is incredible! Although on the first night, you might feel a bit uneasy. The closer to South Africa you get, the more difficult it becomes to camp in the wild outdoors. Most farmers will allow you to camp on their land upon request. Always ask before you put your tent up on someone's land!

Animals

Of course, there are lots of wild animals in Africa and it's amazing to be able to camp around them! It's perfectly safe to camp where there are wild animals, as long as you use common sense.

The first time you hear the sound of snapping twigs as an animal passes by, or the laugh of a hyena, you will probably end up with something unpleasant in your pants. But you will soon get used to it and start enjoying the sounds of the animals around you, while lying in the safety of your rooftop tent.

The sound of snapping twigs, laughing hyenas, trumpeting elephants ... It leads to a mix of terror and excitement and we loved to lay in our rooftop tent and listen to the wild all around us.
—Dries

A Few Things to Consider While Camping in the Wild:

Don't leave your rubbish outside; this will attract animals such as hyenas. Especially if they smell meat.

The same for dirty dishes. Fair enough if you don't feel like doing your dishes after a magnificent braai (South African word for BBQ, as you'll soon learn), but put them in the car.

The same goes for your table. We heard a story about a couple who had put a massive steak on the braai. During preparation, the meat juice had run into the cracks of their table and they didn't clean it up. The next morning, they woke up to find part of their table eaten by hyenas. So like your mother always told you, **wipe the table after every meal**!

If you plan to camp in an area where there are elephants, **lock your citrus fruit in airtight boxes**. Apparently, elephants LOVE citrus and will break a window if they smell it. So put them in your fridge to be safe.

Don't camp next to wildlife trails. You will easily recognise them—paths with a wide range of different animal prints. Don't park on them either, as you will be blocking their 'road' and they won't appreciate it. You will see more of these trails near water sources. Most animals make their way to the water source when the day ends.

Stay close to your car and use a light when it's dark. It's only common sense not to go for a walk in the bush without a light source. Wild animals aren't actually that interested in people and will more likely be scared of you; there is no reason for them to come close to your car as you make a lot of noise and they are scared of noises. If you have to go to the toilet and aren't feeling comfortable getting out of your tent in the dark, the Uri bag is a perfect option for midnight wee-wees.

Don't forget: **don't** feed wild animals!

The first time you see monkeys, they seem really cute and fascinating. You spend hours taking pictures and OMG! How sweet! They will even take a banana out of your hand!

Please, please, don't! After the first rush of love, you will begin to see their real nature—little thieving bastards! Sorry about the language, but during our trip, we learnt to dislike (almost hate) monkeys! If these little rotters are around, close all vehicle doors and windows. If you don't, they will get in and steal whatever they see. In more touristic places, monkeys will steal out of a woman's hand, but they're scared of men! So please, **don't** feed the monkeys, and guys, keep an eye out for your woman!

I once fed a monkey during our trip. It was the first monkey we had seen and it was so cute and so interesting to see one close up. We soon discovered what a very very bad idea this was, when the entire troupe started stealing everything out of our car ... You should learn from your mistakes, right?
—Eef

10

Eco-/Ethical Tourism

The principles of eco-tourism and ethical tourism can overlap, but ethical tourism focuses specifically on people. Eco-tourism concentrates on protection of the environment, without taking the people involved into consideration. It's all well and good when a new resort is built using sustainable means and, in doing so, minimises harm to the environment, but if that same resort has harassed or even displaced communities in order to be built, then it has not been a very ethical venture. Such terms as 'green', 'eco' and 'sustainable' are used in profusion, when in fact they are nothing more than a marketing tool in a number of cases. It is never enough to accept the use of these terms at face value. If you are concerned about ethical travel, you need to be confident that you are not implicated in harmful practices. In fact, to travel ethically, you must go beyond the norm and absolutely ensure that your trip is of benefit to both the places and people you visit.

The greatest part of the tourism industry is owned and controlled by 'outsiders' and because of this, the greatest part of the tourism-based revenue can entirely bypass local communities; this can lead to feelings of resentment and anger, preventing important cultural exchanges, which for many are the very reason for which they travel. Tourists don't ever consciously want to cause harm, but do so unwittingly, through a lack of knowledge and awareness.

Tourism Concern

Tourism Concern is a registered charity that exposes tourism's worst human rights abuses and campaigns against them. Equally importantly, they promote tourism that benefits local communities at tourist destinations.

A big part of what they do at Tourism Concern is to facilitate and encourage that awareness for both the industry and travellers, so people can make better and more informed choices.

Their website is a very useful resource to find information about what to avoid and how to travel correctly. You can read up on and get involved in their campaigns; they publish a list of companies they endorse. Tourism Concern is a member-based organization, so if you do support and share their concerns and efforts, please support them by becoming a member. www.tourismconcern.org.uk

They are currently working hard to develop an ethical travel map—to list places around the world, be it tour companies, restaurants or places to stay—that are bringing real benefits to the local communities, socially, economically and environmentally. These places are small and therefore don't have the marketing budgets to advertise themselves. Tourism Concern tries to promote such places in order to help them thrive through tourism. You can find the Ethical Travel Map online. Please at least take a look and if, when travelling, you discover places you think should be listed, let them know, or encourage the locals to apply via the website: www.tourismconcern.org.uk/ethical-travel-guide

11

Sleeping

In or on the vehicle is the question here. Because of space issues, we opted for a rooftop tent and we have to admit that we slept better in this than in any hotel bed! At the start, we needed time to get used to the technique of setting it up, but once you've done this a few times, it takes approximately one minute to get it out and five minutes to pack it away.

There are various forms, sizes and weights. We chose the Eeziawn 140, which was more than large enough for two.

What to Look For in a Rooftop Tent

- Make sure that the base of the tent is made from wood and not aluminium. We met a couple who had the aluminium version and they had to dry their mattress every morning because it was soaked through. Wood can breathe and in doing so, prevents your mattress from becoming damp overnight.
- Make sure that there are zips and Velcro

fastenings wherever there are holes. **All** gaps need to be easily sealed.

Our model had a front door which was zipped on both sides, but the zips didn't come all the way down to the bottom, leaving a small hole through which the local mosquito population quickly (and happily) realised was a made-to-measure entrance! We solved this by plugging the gaps with items of clothing.

We just LOVED our rooftop tent! It was the best bed ever! Whenever we slept in another bed (with a friend, at a hotel), it was hard to fall asleep. But as soon as our heads touched our pillows in our rooftop tent, we were down for the count!
—Dries

Extra Small Tent

What we later also found useful was an additional small tent.

This way, if you stay somewhere for a few days and plan on regular small trips, or if you go out for a few days hiking, you won't always have to fold up the rooftop tent and pack everything in the car and you won't be completely tied to your vehicle. Sleeping in the small tent before going for an early morning drive to watch the sunrise or animals as they make their way to the waterholes, means you don't have to wake up even earlier in order to pack everything away.

Duvet

If you tend to travel for a long time, it's so much nicer to sleep under a big two-person duvet than in a sleeping bag. It's much more comfortable when you're travelling with your partner.

Are you thinking, 'duvet? In Africa? It's too hot!' Well, you're wrong. It can get bloody cold there!

And when it does get too hot, just take the duvet out of the cover and simply slip under the cover.

Pillowcases

Always put two pillowcases over each pillow.

Africa is always dusty and when it's hot, you sweat. In no time at all, your pillow (even under the cases) will look very dirty (and disgusting). A second pillowcase will protect your pillow just that little bit longer.

Sleeping Bags

We had our sleeping bags with us and they came in quite handy.

Firstly, because we sometimes couch-surfed and it's nice to have your own bedding when sleeping on someone's couch. And secondly, you will sometimes be invited to spend the night at someone's home; strangers, family, friends who have immigrated, etc. So it's nice to save them the trouble of looking for extra bedding. And last of all, if you end up in a place where it's really, really cold, you can use your sleeping bag as an extra layer.

We used ours quite a few times.

12

Photography

You will take thousands of photos during your trip—lots and lots and lots!

The number one rule is to ASK before taking a picture. Please, please, *always* ask people before you take their picture. Some people will love getting their picture taken (especially children), but some people don't like it at all and will find it very insulting to be snapped as they are washing their undies or riding their donkey. People are not tourist attractions. Locals are—on the whole—simply living their lives.

How would we like it, back home? How would you like it if a complete stranger took a picture of you washing the dishes or watching a movie?

So always ask permission. A lot of them will say yes, quite a few of them will say no. Show respect.

Africa gave us some magnificent photo opportunities. It's still such a raw continent and has so many unknown places and hidden beauty. We found ourselves in places where 'whites' were almost unknown. Once, a child ran away when I took out my camera—she thought it would hurt her.
—Eef

What Type of Camera

We can't advise you on makes and models, but we had twocameras with us—a big one and a small one!

In some areas, we didn't feel right walking around with the big camera; we looked like big-ass tourists when we actually wanted to blend in a bit more. Instead of showing off and attracting unwanted attention with a big, expensive camera, we would have the little camera in our pocket, just in case the right opportunity came up.

We had a small camera which we used in places where a larger model would have been the wrong choice. As we didn't use it that often, we forgot to transfer our pictures onto the computer. When the small camera got stolen, we lost some amazing photographs from some equally amazing trips.
—Eef

Backing Up Your Pictures
Save Them

Make sure you save your pictures on a *very* regular basis!

We know it's annoying to transfer your pictures to a computer every time. But if your camera gets stolen, it will have been worth the bother!

Twice

It's not only important to save your pictures, but also important to save them twice, at two different locations. You never know when your laptop will crash. Imagine that, all your pictures ... gone forever!

We always saved them on our computer and on an external hard drive, and then we kept the external hard drive hidden in a place other than our laptop, just in case someone broke in. That way, they might not take all our pictures. Those who prefer to use cloud technology will find computer cafés in larger towns and cities where you can upload your pictures, but often the upload speeds are incredibly slow. For your thousands of pictures, this probably won't be an option.

Send Them Home

We regularly sent our pictures home on flash drives, just in case. We didn't want to risk losing any of the beautiful pictures of our awesome adventure ever again!

Spare Battery

Make sure you bring a spare battery and get into the habit of charging your empty battery as soon as possible. You won't always have electricity and charging a battery while driving takes longer than charging it at home.

Government Buildings and Employees

Never take pictures of official buildings or those working in them. Again, ASK if you want to take a picture of a guard or policeman. You can get into a lot of trouble if you try to sneak a snap, or take a picture when at a border crossing.

Dust, Dust, Dust

We can't warn you enough about the sheer quantities of dust you will encounter on your trip, so try to keep your camera as dust-free as possible. We kept our camera in a bag and in a dust-proof box when we weren't using it. We also made sure that we regularly cleaned the camera with a little brush and used our air compressor on it, too.

13

What to Take

An unwritten rule is, don't bring too much! You will nearly always source what you need during your trip and often at much lower prices than you would pay back home. After three months on the road, we had given away a lot of what we had brought with us. We found out, by trial and error, that we either didn't use some items at all, or that we didn't really need them.

Should you realise that you have brought too much with you, give things away as presents when you are invited to someone's home, or simply leave unnecessary items on the side of the road. Someone will find your discarded treasure and get a lot of pleasure out of this unexpected windfall.

Clothes
General
Again, the rule of thumb is **don't bring too much**! You will have to do a weekly wash to keep up your supply of socks and undies anyway. If you need new clothes, you will find them everywhere at prices much, much lower than back

home. Africa is full of markets selling every item you can imagine and clothes will be easy to find.

For example, in Uganda, we came across a gigantic clothes market, with clothes lying in great piles which you could scrabble your way through looking for something you liked. Every few minutes, the owner would turn a pile over so you could see the clothes that were at the bottom of the pile. These clothes are all second-hand and often brought in from Europe—like the ones you put into clothes' containers at home. These 'donated' clothes are big business and not actually used for charitable means. They are also extremely cheap. If you don't like the idea of wearing second-hand clothes, walking around a market like this is still a great experience.

Should you realise that you have too many clothes with you (like me), keep the clothes you don't immediately need in a box for later. After a while, your current outfits will fade, rip and stretch through constant sun, constant washing and constant adventure. This way, you'll just be able to open the box for a fresh, colourful change.

Don't bring anything **white**! Even a T-shirt with a small, white print won't look clean for long; tiny white dots or lines on undies will never be white again! A lot of underwear is white and no matter how much you scrub them, they will never regain their sparkle. You will look like you are wearing dirty underwear all the time, which isn't such a great feeling!

It appears that tsetse flies are attracted to dark colours, especially black and (dark) blue. You will meet tsetse flies whenever you go on safari, in thick vegetation and in rural areas, so try to avoid darker colours, and don't wear black or dark blue in these areas.

Tsetse flies are hosts to the parasite that causes sleeping sickness (trypanosomiasis). There are no preventive measures or vaccinations for sleeping sickness. Symptoms are: a painful, small ulcer at the bite site, high fever, painful headaches and muscle pain. Although the risk of contracting the disease is low, you should be aware that the flies carrying this parasite are mainly to be found in rural areas and in dense vegetation. When in such areas or when on safari, wear long sleeves and trousers and bring insect repellent. Don't let tsetse flies spoil your adventures, be prepared. We never encountered any tsetse-related problems and never worried about them, either.

100% cotton clothes will not dry so quickly after washing.

And remember: jeans are hot when it's hot, cold when it's cold and wet when it's wet.

Women's Clothes

One important rule when it comes to clothing—especially for women—is to **respect the local culture**! Always research the customs and habits of the area you will be travelling in. Always ask for advice, or look at what the locals themselves are wearing. In general, woman in the north of Africa should cover their shoulders. As you travel further south, uncovered shoulders become more acceptable. Skirts must always fall below the knee. We often saw tourists walking around in way-too-short shorts and it made us pretty angry. Dressing this way shows a complete lack of respect. I always wore long skirts, and often got compliments from the local women. They would say that they liked my clothes much more than what they saw the 'tourists' wear. **Lightweight long skirts and maxi-dresses** are a great choice for travelling through Africa. They show your respect to the local community and will mean your presence will be even more appreciated.

They don't take up much space, will protect you from the sun, and they look great, too!

Skirts are always useful, as you will come across a lot of 'squat' toilets in Africa and the last thing you want to do is let your trousers fall into the murky puddles around you. Another option would be **trousers elasticated around the knees, calves or ankles**.

As you will mainly be camping and will need to change clothes in the open, a skirt is the best choice making it easy to switch underwear or pull on a pair of trousers without giving other campers or curious locals a free show.

You might find it useful to bring along a knee length **strapless dress** (see picture) to use for the shower. Most showers are small and without any hooks to hang your clothes on. You won't want to either stand completely naked or place your clothes on the ground.

Wearing a strapless dress, with nothing else underneath, means you can have a shower, walk back to your camp and get dressed again with ease and more importantly, without giving a free peep show. And there's an added bonus. If you buy one with an elastic bodice (as shown in the picture), you can also use it as a skirt.

I always have found it difficult to store my bra's properly during our trip. But I have now found this amazing **bra travel case**, formed in the shape of a bra and very sturdy, so your bras will keep their shape on the road.

Laundry

You will have to hand wash your clothes on the road. A great trick is to bring along a bucket with a tight-fitting lid. You can find these at rowboat suppliers, as rowers need a bucket in the boat to keep things dry should they capsize. Put your dirty clothes in the bucket with some soap and water and tie it to the roof. A day's driving on African 'roads' will mean you have a very ecological and very efficient washing machine in your kit. Once at a campsite, rinse your clothes and hang out to dry, and you've saved yourself a lot of (very boring) work.

If you wash by hand, you will probably use more soap on the sweaty parts (underarms). Turn your T-shirt inside out to wash these areas; otherwise you will end up with discolorations in these spots.

When you finish washing your clothes, you should try to get the clothes as dry as possible before hanging. Squeeze instead of wring; wringing will ruin your clothes much faster. And wringing isn't good for the wrist joints, either.

A final tip. When you hang your clothes out to dry, hang them inside out. This not only means they will be less discoloured by the bleaching effect of the sun, but if a bird flies over, at least the poop won't be visible on the outside.

Two years travelling through Africa has made us hand-washing experts! But I can still remember how hard it was in the beginning: sore hands, damaged skin and hours of scrubbing. We were also surprised how dirty our clothes were; the water would turn brown almost immediately ... really brown! I'm not sure if we ever really got that dust out of our clothes.
—Eef

Electronics
Additional Phone

An extra mobile phone or a mobile phone with dual SIM is convenient. Calling or sending texts in Africa with a foreign SIM card is quite expensive, so it is better to buy a local SIM card when you want to call campsites, the immigration office, etc. Local SIM cards are easy to obtain and inexpensive.

E-reader

When you're travelling by car with a very limited amount of space, a full load of books is unfortunately not an option. Purchase an e-reader (preferably two to avoid unnecessary fights) and you can carry an entire library with you. Even if you're not a big reader, you will be amazed by the number of books you'll read while on the move.

Power Bank

You can use a power bank to recharge your phone and e-reader. Some need a short time to recharge or top up.

Additional Hard Drive

Take an extra hard drive with you to back up your photo collection. Keep it in a different place than your laptop. If your laptop is stolen, you won't lose your memories.

Movies

At times, it can be pretty cold and it's no fun to sit outside at night. Enjoy the luxury of a movie night in the tent.

Solar Energy

If there is one thing that you can be sure of in Africa, it is the sun, so solar-charged energy is the way to go. Often, solar-charging lights and chargers will also incorporate a cigarette lighter adaptor so you can also charge while driving, if you want.

Magnetic Light

As your house is a vehicle and the vehicle is primarily made of metal, magnetic lights can come in very handy.

They are great to stick in the vehicle if you are looking for something in low light levels, or on the outside of the vehicle when having dinner. You can even stick them under the car when doing check-ups or maintenance.

USB
Use a USB port with cigarette lighter adaptor so phones and e-readers can be charged while driving.

Head Torches
Super handy!

Dark in Africa means really, REALLY dark! You won't find a lot of lighting on camping grounds and obviously you won't find any if you've made your own bush camp.

So a head torch comes in very handy when doing the dishes, walking to the toilet, brushing your teeth, etc.

Navigator
We consider this an absolute necessity!

Dongle
Nowadays, everyone uses a smartphone to access the Internet. For that small percentage of people who don't use one, there is the 'dongle'. This is a flash drive which accepts a SIM card and can then be plugged into your computer to access the Internet. We used it during our trip (you can buy one in Ethiopia, Kenya, etc.). Insert a local SIM card and every time you cross a border, buy a new local SIM card (very cheap) for further Internet access. It works in the same way as the SIM card for your phone.

Plugs
Every country has a different plug connection, so you will

need different adaptors for each country. There are really good travel adapters on the market which you can swap over according to the plug shape required. Alternatively, you will easily find adaptors at local stores in each country you visit and they're pretty cheap.

In the chapters relating to specific countries, I refer to electrical plugs using 'TYPE'. These types are world standards.

Type C

Egypt, Ethiopia,
Zambia, South Africa

Type D

Sudan, Tanzania,
Zambia, Botswana,
Namibia, South Africa

Type F

Ethiopia

Type G

Kenya, Uganda,
Tanzania, Malawi,
Zambia, Botswana

Type M

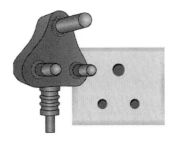

Namibia, South Africa

(Info from www.worldstandards.eu/electricity/plug-voltage-by-country)

Bits and Pieces
Hot Water Bottle

A lot of people don't realise how cold Africa can be and we often found ourselves victims of this error. High places can get damn cold at night, especially when sleeping in the open. We bought a hot water bottle on the road and used it a lot!

> *We never thought it would get very cold in Africa. The first time we realised how wrong we were was in Kenya. We could see our breath in our rooftop tent! It was so cold that we heated up stones in a fire and put them in a sock to heat the bed! Not much later we bought a hot water bottle ... much safer for the mattress.*
> *—Dries*

Click-Seal/Zip-Lock Bags

Travelling overland through Africa means a lot of dust.

Click-seal/zip-lock bags are very handy for protecting things like cameras and other electronics.

Photo Album/Pictures

During our trip, we found that many of the people we met wanted to know what our homeland looked like, what kind of foods we ate, who our family were ... Make a small photo album before you leave with pictures of family, friends, pets, your favourite foods and what your home country looks like. Keep it within easy reach. You will find that the album is extremely appreciated, especially when there's a language barrier. It can keep any 'conversation' going!

In some African countries, English isn't considered a second or even a third language and although the locals really, really want to help you, it can be hard work explaining what you need.

For example, we couldn't find a way to describe our rooftop tent. It was almost impossible! They understood the concept; we needed to find place to sleep, but we already had a tent. But they couldn't understand that the tent stayed on top of the car and we weren't simply able to put up our tent in their tiny courtyard. So we ended up searching for and printing out a picture of an open rooftop tent. If we ever make a similar trip again, we will definitely bring along a picture of an open rooftop tent.

Small Gifts

On your journey, you will often be invited to pop over for a cup of tea, to have a meal, to spend the night, etc. Make sure you bring a small gift in return. A toy for the kids or a photo of yourselves is really appreciated. Don't give money, as this can be insulting and might upset their natural hospitality.

Name Cards

It is always useful to have name cards printed with your email address, website, Facebook page, etc. You can give these to other travellers and people you meet along the way, so you can stay in contact.

TIP

Design and print these yourself (four per page) on photographic paper. It works out a lot cheaper and you can easily make more on the road when you run out!

Aluminium Drinking Bottle

It's great to have cold water close at hand when driving. The fridge (if you decide to bring one) is often in the back of the vehicle and difficult to reach. We had a Haglöfs aluminium drinking bottle and the water stayed cold for almost the entire day! There are probably other great makes out there, but we were more than happy with Haglöfs. These are also handy when going for an early walk drive, as they will keep your coffee or tea warm.

We hadn't used the bottle that one of our sponsors (Haglöfs) had given us during our first five months of travelling. But one day we decided to use it and put some water in it. OMG! That water stayed cold for the entire day! Wish we had used that bottle from the start.
—Dries

Sleeping Mask and Ear Plugs

Depending on how easily you fall asleep and how deeply you sleep, these might be worth bringing along. In some countries, there is a mosque on every corner that will reverberate with loud calls to prayer at the most unsociable of hours. Ear plugs will make a real difference! Some campsites offer public lighting, but often these lights are aimed right onto your tent. If you can only sleep when it's dark, bring a sleeping mask with you. You'll be glad you did.

Small Brush
So handy to wipe the sand out your car (or your bed!).

Games
You will be travelling in a very small group (partner, friend, family). Living together 24/7 in the confines of a small vehicle will use up any conversation you have within the first few weeks, so bring some games along.

We brought a few games with us. Some were really good, some were really bad. Here are the ones we loved, which you can play with just two people: Rummikub, Qwirkle, Caesar and Yahtzee.

Sewing Kit
A friend of ours gave us the tiniest sewing kit we had ever seen. We hadn't even considered getting one ourselves, so we just stuffed it in a corner of our vehicle. We ended up being really glad we brought it along, because we used it a lot! Fixing a hole in a shirt, putting a button back on a pair of trousers, repairing a loose stitch on one of our camping chairs and even stitching Eef's flip-flop—yes, a flip-flop. We'd never seen it done before, but in Africa, they will stitch plastic, flip-flops, plastic containers ... so we tried it ourselves. It works brilliantly!

Bring a sewing kit, or just a few needles and some thread, and you'll be good for the next few years!

Bird Book

Africa has amazing wildlife: elephants, zebras, lions, giraffes, etc. But apart from the big boys, it also has amazingly beautiful and colourful birdlife! During our trip, we bought a bird book and used it almost every day. You will see such an amazing variety of birds.

(After a while, zebras and giraffes become an everyday sight, so it was nice to get excited about something new.)

(Bicycle) Inner Tube

This might sound strange, but you've no idea about how useful an inner tube can be!

We took two with us and used them all the time! Inner tubes are soft, flexible and elastic. They are perfect to tie something, such as firewood, onto the roof; hold the broken cupboard doors closed when the locking mechanism fails; etcetera, etcetera, etcetera.

14

Useful Apps

If you have a smartphone, there are some very useful apps that you can make use of during your trip.

Here are a few examples of the ones we found most useful:

Facebook Pages
Free, app, website

We all know about Facebook. Set up a page dedicated to your travels that others can follow. It's easy to upload pictures and write updates using the smartphone app.

Spending Tracker
Free, app

We've tried a few apps to keep track of our expenses and we found this one to be the best.

You can fill in your expenses and sort them by category and the app will give you an overview of your weekly/monthly/ yearly expenses, either in a list or with pictographs.

It also allows you to set a budget to show you what part of your budget is left.

This is a free app, but if you upgrade to the Pro version for €0.99, it allows you to make backups directly to your Dropbox, or export your expenses in CSV or PDF format so you can email them to yourself.

This way, if your phone dies or gets stolen or lost, your expenses are still listed elsewhere.

iOverlander
Free, app, website

The app version of their website.

iOverlander is a database of all places of interest for overlanders; camping sites, petrol stations, mechanics, restaurants, etc.

Details are entered by other travellers. You can also see how old the listing is.

Each entry includes details such as address, amenities, GPS coordinates, reviews, etc.

You can browse through a list or use a map. You can open up a specific location in other map apps such as Google Maps or Maps.me for directions.

The great thing about this app is that you can use it offline! (Very handy in Africa).

Make sure you also add some of your own listings while on the road. After all, this is an app by overlanders for overlanders!

Maps.me
Free, app, website

Maps.me provides maps from all over the world!

The best thing about this app is that you can download maps of a specific region or country and use them offline.

Maps are interactive—you can add your own favourite places or even open points of interest from iOverlander (see above) and get directions.

TripAdvisor
Free, app, website

Everyone knows Tripadvisor.com, so this one doesn't need much of an explanation.

I've found Tripadvisor.com to only be useful for more touristic places, but it can be extremely handy in cities to check reviews about restaurants and hotels and to look up nearby activities. It's used more by tourists than overlanders, though.

Couchsurfing
Free, app, website

We love couch-surfing.

Using this app, you can find a free couch (sometimes bed) in someone's home.

It's the perfect way to meet new and local people. We totally recommend it!

You can also read reviews from people who have stayed with a particular person previously.

We don't always use it to find a place to sleep, but simply as a way to meet local people to show us around and take us to places well off the beaten track.

Airbnb

Free, app, website

We only used this app in cities.

In bigger cities, it's often hard to find a decent campsite.

You might have run into some bad luck (a breakdown, a rainstorm) and just need a bed for the night.

Airbnb is a great alternative to hotels or hostels and often offers much better value!

At Airbnb, people with a spare room open up their home to you, so once again, it's a nice way to meet local people.

If you don't want to rent a room in someone's house, some people also rent out entire properties (flats/houses/bungalows).

XE

Free, app, website

XE is a free currency converter that you can also use offline.

The moment you go online, it updates all currency exchange rates.

Duolingo
Free, app, website

Duolingo is a free and fun app for learning a language.

Lessons are very easy and made into a kind of a game. It makes learning a new language—or at least the basics—easy and fun. You can use the full version when connected to the internet. The app will also load a few lessons that you can use when offline.

It provides courses for the most common languages, including Swahili.

If you want to practice before you go, they also have a website.

Memrise
Free, app, website

Another language learning app, but with more languages and better offline quality.

The app includes Swahili, basic Arabic and Afrikaans.

Google Translate
Free, app, website

This might be handy if you need a direct translation of a specific word or simple phrase.

SkyView
Free, app

Definitely not a must, but it's fun.

SkyView is an app that will show you the stars and star signs when you hold your phone up to the sky. It's pretty impressive. Unfortunately, it won't work offline.

Games

It's always nice to have a few games, just for the long drives.

There are plenty out there, but make sure you choose ones that you can play offline.

15

The End

That sad day has arrived. Your trip has come to an end. You have reached South Africa. You made it. Congratulations! Hooray! (Obviously, this chapter is only for those overlanders travelling north to south).

You reached the final destination. Now what do you do with your vehicle?

Selling

You can always sell your vehicle. Here are two companies that can help you when selling your car:

Expedition Trucks
www.expedition-trucks.com

Expedition Truck Brokers specialises in trucks and can help you sell your truck anywhere in the world.

Africa 4x4 Café
www.africa4x4cafe.com

Enzo at Africa 4x4 Café will give you hand when trying to sell your car anywhere in the world. He can also store vehicles.

Shipping
African Overlanders

African Overlanders is based in Stellenbosch. Duncan is an ex-overlander.

He is the guy to go to if you have any car-related problems in Africa and will most likely help you out or at least point you in the right direction.

He also provides accommodation (camping plots and rooms) at his place, so you can stay there while preparing both yourselves and your vehicle for shipping.

You can get your car shipped back home in a container. There are two options:

- A 20ft container (one car)
- A 40ft container (two cars)

The advantage of the 40ft container is that your shipping costs will be 25% cheaper. The disadvantage is that you will have to find someone with whom to share the container.

We went for the 40ft container and stored our car with Duncan until he found a container mate for us. In 2015, we paid US$2,800.

To get a quote or for more information have a look at their website at: www.africanoverlanders.com.

Storage

You might want to return to Africa, as you've enjoyed the experience so much. There are a few places to store your car, but we've only used one.

African Overlanders

African Overlanders provides three storage options on their wireless-alarm-system-protected compound.

Outside:

Car: R400/month
Bike: R200/month
Big trucks/trailers: R600/month

Under Cover (Shade Cloth):

Car: R500/month
Bike: R300/month
Big trucks/trailers: R600/month

Container Storage:

(Max height 2.56 m and must be pre-ordered)

Car: R700/month
Bike: R400/month

Prices includes storage, fortnightly engine start, tyre pressure check, battery charging when necessary and a fire insurance policy of R2 million (you can opt out of this insurance and save R100 per car/truck and R50 per bike).

You will need to pay three months' storage in advance and the remainder upon your return.

You will find more information on their website:

www.africanoverlanders.com

Countries

An Introduction

In the following chapters, we will go into more detail about the countries we've been through, giving you a bit of general information, our personal experiences, our favourite campsites and restaurants and so on.

We travelled through Africa between 2013 and 2015, so of course things might have changed: campsites might have closed, restaurants might have changed chefs/menus or be under new management, so we can't help it if this is the case. We just hope they have stayed the same, so you can experience our favourite places, too.

You can also find a full list of all the campsites we've been to on our website (www.whereismistercarrot.com) in 'The Traveller' section.

All prices listed were current when researching this book. You should check more current sources for the most up to date information.

We researched the 'Crossing the Border' sections thoroughly while writing this book, so this information should be up to date, but if we can give you one tip and one tip only, it is this: make sure you know exactly what you need (for both yourself *and* your car) BEFORE entering the country. This will save you a lot of hassle and time.

So now we can only say, enjoy the wealth of countries that lie ahead of you!

Eef and Dries

Index of Ammenities

 Cold Shower

 Flushing Toilet

 Hot Shower

 Squatting Toilet

 Drinkable Water

 Internet

 Non-Drinkable Water

 BBQ

 Electricity

 Swimming Pool

 On-Site Restaurant

 Washing Machine

Europe

Our Experience

We left Belgium and made our way towards Turkey. It was snowing when we left, so we didn't stay at campsites. Instead of booking hotel rooms, we opted for couch-surfing, where we were given the opportunity to meet some amazing people. We also tried, saw and tasted some incredible things. Which is why, we are sorry to say, you won't find any hotel or campsite information in this chapter.

Travelling by Car

Fuel

On www.fuel-prices-europe.info, you can check current European petrol prices. They are updated daily.

The table shows which countries are better for filling up than others.

Country	Unleaded 95/L	Diesel/L
Czech Republic	€ 1.122	€ 1.157
Austria	€ 1.148	€ 1.048
Croatia	€ 1.248	€ 1.168
Bulgaria	€ 1.027	€ 1.022
Serbia	€ 1.196	€ 1.234
Hungary	€ 1.134	€ 1.129
Slovenia	€ 1.279	€ 1.195
Germany	€ 1.379	€ 1.169
Belgium	€ 1.402	€ 1.326
Turkey	€ 1.262	€ 1.112

Prices: September 2017

Bulgaria

Roads

If you plan on driving on the motorway in Bulgaria, you will need to buy a 'vignette'. You can easily purchase these at the border, roadside stores or petrol stations. For a vehicle of up to 3.5 tonnes, you will pay €5/week or €13/month. For a vehicle weighing 3.5–12 tonnes, you will pay €7/day, €18/week or €49/month.

Watch out! Border control will not tell you that you need to purchase a vignette; however, should you not buy one, the police *will* stop you a few miles further on.

Tip
Alcohol is very cheap in Bulgaria.

Turkey

Roads

All toll roads in Turkey work via the 'HGS-system' (fast transit system) and it is no longer possible to pay tolls with cash or credit cards. You need an HGS registration label, or an HGS registration card and you are required to display this on your front windshield/windscreen.

HGS labels or cards can be bought and loaded at the border, at post offices (PTT: yellow and blue logo) and at Shell petrol stations. You can also load cards at toll stations on the motorway.

To purchase an HGS card or label, you need to show your vehicle registration documents and passport and pay TL10. You must load the card with a minimum of TL30 and you will be able to add more credit to it later on.

The HGS label or card incorporates a chip. When passing a toll booth, the sum is automatically calculated and debited and you do not need to stop. After passing a toll booth, you will receive a text on your mobile phone which tells you the amount of credit remaining on your card. When you have too little credit, you may continue to drive, but you have to add money to your card within 14 days.

There are regular controls on approach and exit roads.

Tip
Don't drive through Istanbul during rush hour!

Iskenderun

At Iskenderun, you will find a big shopping mall called 'Prime Mall'. You can buy pretty much everything here.

The local (white) buses cost 2TL for any trip through town.

Egypt

Our Experience

We loved Egypt! All the people were so lovely and welcoming. As local tourism has dropped over the last years, they're very happy to see tourists. Everywhere we walked, people shouted, 'Welcome to Egypt!' It was probably the only English sentence they knew.

Hospitality is taken very seriously here; bring a small gift when they invite you for tea and you will be best friends forever.

The only negative side of Egypt as far as we were concerned was that this was the only country that was extremely difficult and expensive to get in *and* out of.

General Information

Capital: Cairo
Language Spoken: Arabic and English
Population: 93.1 million
Religion: Muslim (mostly Sunni) 90%, Coptic 9%, other Christians 1%
Currency: Egyptian Pound (E£)
ATM: Most ATMs accept all major credit card withdrawals, including Visa and MasterCard
Electricity: 220V, European two-pin round, Type C
Climate: Egypt is hot during the entire year except for the months of December, January and February.
Time Zone: UTC +2
Country Code: +20
Shops: Markets and small shops

Visa

Visas are required for all nations, except those coming from Arab countries.

Cost: US$25
Validity: 30 days
Where to Get One: You should get a visa from the Egyptian embassy or consulate in your country prior to departure.

Travelling by Car

Carnet

We needed a carnet, but recently (September 2016) the FIA (Federation International de l' Automobile) confirmed that Egypt has changed the rules, meaning foreigners do not require a carnet upon entry. Such things can change quickly, so keep an eye out on forums and on the Overland Association information page (overlandingassociation.org/carnet-de-passage).

If you do need to get paperwork done, it's worth employing a 'fixer' who can help you with the entire procedure. You can try to do it yourself, but it will cost you both a lot of time (and we mean A LOT) and a lot of effort.

Driving

Drive on the right side of the road.

Road Conditions

In general, the tarmac roads are good, but expect to see some crazy driving, especially in the bigger cities.

Police

Expect to be stopped a lot by the police. However, we found the police in Egypt to be very friendly and helpful—we even spent a night at a police station when we couldn't find a place to stay. During our time in Egypt, the country was going through a rough patch, with a big drop in tourism as a consequence of this. The people were therefore very happy to see us and really took care of us. We even had to leave our mobile phone number at a local police station and they often called to check on how we were doing. We even got an escort for half a day! This might sound a bit scary, but we never felt unsafe at any time.

Fuel

The fuel in the north (Port Said) is extremely cheap, so top up here! As you travel south, it can become very hard to find diesel—we once had to wait eight hours to fill up, so make sure you top up wherever you can and make sure you know how far it is to the next petrol station.

Car help

Toyota Egypt—New Cairo Service Center

Address: Cairo Festival City - Meeting V New Cairo
Phone: +20 (0)16 550
Website: www.ToyotaEgypt.com.eg

Crossing the Border

Turkey–Egypt

Due to politics, it's hard to get into Egypt with your car. One day the ferry will be open, the next day it will be closed. So it's important to keep an eye on the forums for more up-to-date information.

We took the Iskenderun (Turkey)–Port Said (Egypt) ferry, but this one is out of action at the time of writing. We still include this information because by the time of publishing, the ferry might be running again. This is Egypt, after all.

Ferry from Iskenderun (Turkey) to Port Said (Egypt)

Taking the ferry is a big adventure, worth the experience.

This is where your patience will be put to the test—and good preparation for what you are about to experience throughout Africa. Booking the ferry in Turkey by yourself is simple enough, but getting your car off the boat and—more importantly—out of the port in Egypt is a different matter. It is best to use a 'fixer' for this purpose. A 'fixer' is a person who knows the whole procedure: what papers are needed, what people need to be contacted, etc. More information below!

Turkey

You need to book at Remon Travel—this is the only agency that does this in Iskenderun.

> **Remon Travel**
> **Address:** 16 Zemin Kat – Iskenderun
> **Email:** info@remontur.com
> **Website:** www.remontur.com
> **Phone:** +90 (0)850 840 9580
> **Price:** US$550 per car (<5 metres)
> US$180 per person

The ferry normally leaves on Saturdays, but because of weather conditions and problems at the port, we were only able to leave on the Tuesday. If you're in a hurry, best check by emailing them or giving them a call. There is a lady there who speaks fairly good English.

The Day of Departure

Let's give you a little overview about how our day went:

9:30–10:40 a.m. At the agency (time spent waiting).

11 a.m. Arrival at the port; they come and collect your passports. Men and women's passports are taken by separate officials.

2 p.m. Eef gets her passport back.

2:30 p.m. Official comes to check our luggage in the car and takes the vehicle documentation so he can make up papers for the car

3:30 p.m. Dries gets his passport back.

5 p.m. We get the papers back for the car.

5:30 p.m. Drive car onto boat.

8:30 p.m. Boat leaves port.

When you board the boat, you have to go to the reception area to hand in your passport. They will keep it until you arrive in Egypt and arrange your visa (no one told us that).

The boat is very nice. You get a lot of free (and tasty) food, tea and water on the first deck. The floors to the toilets can get a bit wet. (For photos and more about our adventure on the boat, please have a look at our website www. whereismistercarrot.com.)

At 6:45 p.m. the next day, we arrived in Port Said (25 hrs 15 min. on the boat).

Egypt
6:45 p.m. Boat arrives at port.

We go downstairs to drive the car off the boat. The 'fixer' is waiting for us (we had emailed him beforehand).

Return to get our passport back. (Visa: €20 pp; cheaper for us because we paid in Euros.)

9 p.m. Left the boat for a second time.

Get luggage in car checked.

Go and park car in secured parking space (as it's already late, they will only start with the papers for the car tomorrow).

10:20 p.m. Finally, able to leave the port—but without the car!

Our fixer asked for the car keys—he said he needed them to start the paperwork. We were very tired, but as he kept on going about the car keys we gave them to him. Nothing was stolen, but if we were to do this again, we wouldn't give him the car keys.

The next day, we met up with our fixer and got our keys back. In general, it takes 3–4 days to get the car out of the port, but because of problems in Port Said, it took seven days. Nevertheless, we met some incredible people in Port Said and had an unforgettable time!

The 'Fixer'

You need a fixer to get through the border. I don't think you would be able to do this by yourself as only a few people working at the port speak English and our fixer paid a lot under the table to get the car processed faster (which was still 3–4 days). If you try to do everything yourself, we have no idea how long it would take.

We contacted our fixer by email before arriving at the port to secure a price. You should also send him pictures of the car, both inside and out, as ours ended up charging us more because we had built a cupboard in our car.

He responded very quickly to our initial emails, but when we tried to call him, he didn't answer. Once we had hired him, communication became a bit difficult. However, he did his job.

Details

Due to reasons of privacy, we can't share his details, but if the ferry runs again, we are sure you will be able to find his details on one of the forums.

Price (2013)

> **E£3,000** for the fixer
> **E£770** Delivery order from agent to customs
> **E£50** Customs clearance. For this, you have to go to the police station. Make sure you bring copies of your passport. It's a bit of a hassle, but as you have to wait to get the car out of the port anyway, you have the time to figure this part out yourself. You will need to pay E£50 at the police station.

We also had to pay an extra E£200 for parking fees as our car had to stay longer than expected. It usually only takes three to four days to get the car out of the port, but as there were protests going on at the time we were there, we ended up having to wait for seven.

Our Recommendations

There are a lot of hotels and camping is often allowed on the hotel grounds if you ask beforehand, especially in rural areas where campsites are not common.

Wadi El-Hitan (Valley of the Whales)

Things to See

Wadi El-Hitan National Park

Coordinates: N29° 15.858' E30° 01.343'

Wadi El-Hitan is part of the Wadi El-Rayan Protected Area. It's a World Heritage Site with whale skeletons—whale skeletons in the middle of the desert!! Very impressive and worth going and having a look!

Wadi El-Rayan Protected Area

Beautiful waterfalls in the middle of the desert.

Coordinates: N29° 11.840' E30° 22.637'

Camping

Wadi El-Hitan

Coordinates: N29° 15.858' E30° 01.343'
Price: E£80

There is a little kind of 'hut' where you pay, then they point out the camping area to you—anywhere in the surrounding desert! Camping in the middle of the desert is absolutely magnificent!

Aswan

If you need help in Aswan for any reason (finding an embassy for your passport, problem with your car, etc.) you can contact our friend Emad (+20 (0)1117710763 or +20 (0)1220173302). He is a local taxi driver in Aswan and helped us out brilliantly whenever we were stuck.

Camping
Adam's Home

> **Coordinates:** N24° 10.135' E32° 51.971'
> **Price:** E£70 (2 adults in a car)
> **Address:** Garb, Aswan, Egypt
> **Phone:** +20 (0)12 244 21767
> **Facebook:** www.facebook.com/adamhome.camp

Owners Sami and Mohamed offer a campsite and accommodations in mud-brick rooms in a traditional Nubian house, located on the west bank of the Nile, north of Aswan, near the new bridge across the river. The campsite itself is basically a parking area and there is no shade, but it does have showers and toilets. Mohamed, who speaks English, can be contacted on: +20(0)12 244 21 767.

How to Reach It
You can find Adam's Home by driving north along the Nile road from Aswan, then make a left onto the new Aswan suspension bridge. After crossing the bridge, turn right and go underneath it; you will then be on the Garb Aswan road.

Continue for about 2.5 km (1.55 miles) until you get to the first Nubian Village (Sheikh Mohamed) and you will find Adam's Home Camping and Tourist Holidays on the right, clearly signposted for camping.

Sudan

Our Experience

We really, really enjoyed Sudan; that feeling of complete freedom while driving through the desert, travelling down the road as the sun sets and evening comes, camping in the wilderness—in the pitch dark and under a starry sky. It is simply amazing!

The Sudanese are also very friendly and hospitable people.

Many do not speak English, but be prepared to be invited for tea without any ulterior motives such as money or gifts. Remember that a refusal will be considered to be an insult in Sudan, so when people give you a present or offer you food, always accept the offer graciously.

The Sudanese are so welcoming. You might find yourself in a restaurant, and upon asking for the bill, be told that someone has already paid it for you. This person wants nothing in return and has often disappeared before you are able to thank them. Hospitality is huge here and it takes some getting used to, but enjoy the experience of no-strings-attached!

While in Khartoum, we couch-surfed, which enabled us to get to know the local people. We can't recommend this highly enough. We have met people who took us to places that, as outsiders or tourists, we would never have experienced otherwise.

We still think back on our time in Sudan with a smile and cherish our beautiful memories of this incredible country.

General Information

Capital: Khartoum
Language Spoken: Arabic and English
Population: 40.9 million
Religion: Sunni Muslim 70% (in north), Christian 5% (mostly in south and Khartoum), indigenous beliefs 25%
Currency: Sudanese Pounds (S£)
ATMs: There are no ATMs that will accept foreign bank accounts, so you will have to change money: USD or EUR (preferably USD). You can exchange

money at the bank, but might be better off asking the locals, as you will often find better exchange rates on the street.

Electricity: 230V, Type C and D

Climate: The months from May to September are extremely hot—up to 45 degrees Celsius (113 degrees Fahrenheit). December to mid-March temperatures only reach 40 degrees Celsius (104 degrees Fahrenheit). In the south, most roads will be muddy from April to September.

Time Zone: UTC +3

Country Code: +249

Shops: Small little street stalls for basic products and markets for fresh produce

Visa

A visa is required for all travellers of all nationalities and cannot be obtained at the borders, only at a Sudanese Embassy.

You can obtain a visa in Cairo or Aswan (Egypt), but it's cheaper to obtain the visa in Aswan. We didn't have a letter of invitation for Sudan and they didn't ask for one. We think that the letter might possibly speed up the visa procedure. We did this without a fixer and did not encounter any problems.

Consulate General of the Republic of Sudan in Aswan

Coordinates: N24° 05.5176' E032° 88.3164'

Location: El Sadat Rd. - El Khazzah Rd. (close to the Al Rudwan Mosque), Aswan

Phone: +20 (0)97 230 7231

Requirements: Two passport pictures, copy of your passport and passport
Cost: US$50
Validity: One month
Time to Obtain: Three to five days. Ours took five days. When we arrived to pick it up, the papers were still on the desk where we'd left them and they only started on the visa on our arrival. So in principle, you might be able to get your visa earlier if you turn up in person at an earlier date. We heard from other travellers that it only took them three days. Apparently, it can take up to two weeks for American citizens, as their paperwork has to be processed in Khartoum and therefore has to be sent away.

Travelling by Car

Carnet
You will need a carnet.

Driving
Drive on the right side of the road.

Road Conditions
Generally speaking, the roads are in good condition although they cannot be compared to Western standards. Roads get worse along the Nile and even worse towards the south of Sudan.

Police
We found the police to be very friendly, but there were many road blocks where they insist on checking your papers.

Fuel

It is relatively easy to find petrol/diesel. Just make sure that you always refill when given the opportunity, because you will sometimes be travelling long distances where there are no gas stations to be found.

Crossing the Border

Egypt–Sudan

When we did this crossing in 2013, we had to take the ferry from Aswan (Egypt) to Wadi Halfa (Sudan) and it was one hell of an experience. Nowadays the road is open and you still have to take a ferry, but for a very short voyage. If we ever go again, we will take the road.

As said before, everything can change in the blink of an eye in Africa, so make sure you check for the latest information on websites and forums before you leave!

Below, you can find information about the crossing, which has been written by other travellers. Big thanks to '4-wheel-nomads' and 'Abseitsreisen', who have given us permission to include their information in our book.

Keep in mind that this is a personal experience. It is not a 'how-to' guide and things might be different when you try to cross the border yourself.

Crossing with the Help of a Fixer

By 4-wheel-nomads (4-wheel-nomads.de), end of October 2015
(Translated from German)

We decided to take a fixer for the border procedure although it is also possible to do that on your own.

Our fixer for the Egyptian side, Kamal Muawad, has a very good reputation with overlanders.

These are his contact details:
>**Phone:** +20 (0)100 532 2669
>**Mobile:** +20 (0)122 139 3492
>**Email:** kamalaswanegy@yahoo.com

In Aswan, it is important to go to the transport court (together with the fixer), where checks are made for any outstanding traffic tickets. If you don't have their stamp in your passport and you try to pass the border, the Egyptian border checkpoint will send you back to Aswan.

A visa for Sudan is easy to obtain from the Sudanese Consulate General in Aswan.

Consulate General of the Republic of Sudan
>**Address:** El Sadat Rd. - El Khazzah Rd. (close to the Al Rudwan Mosque) Aswan
>**Phone:** +20 (0)97 230 7231
>**Coordinates:**
>N24° 05.5176' E032° 88.3164'

You don't need a fixer for this, but using one could speed up the process and maybe help extend your visa's validity (US$50 per family).

For the visa application process, you will need:

- Two passport photos
- A photocopy of your passport
- Your passport

The visa application form (they will supply you with one at the consulate) must be fully filled in—in the form, they ask for other valid visas in your possession, so I figured out that it might help to have the **Ethiopian visa** before applying for the one for Sudan. This is easy to get at the Ethiopian Embassy, Consular Section, 21 Sheikh Mohamed El Ghazali Street, Dokki in Cairo. It takes one working day, costs US$60 for one month/one border crossing and US$70 for three months/two crossings.

We also had an invitation letter to Sudan which is not mandatory, but also may help speed up the process.

Usually, the Sudanese visa takes approximately three working days (in our case, it took two). For Americans, it can take up to two weeks as the details have to be sent to Khartoum and processed there.

The price for the Sudan visa application in Aswan is US$50 each (instead of the US$110 charged in Cairo). Usually, you get one month; our visas were valid for two months (due to what, we have no idea).

A good place to stay for overlanders is the Nubian house 'Adam's Home Overland Camp', where you can camp for around E£70 (about €8) for a car and two adults.

Adam's Home Overland Camp
    Coordinates: N24°10.135' E032° 51.971'
    Phone: +20 (0)122 442 1767
    Email: adamhome.camp@facebook.com

It's a great place at the west bank of the Nile (a bit run-down at the moment, though, due to health issues of the owner and the fall in tourism). They can also organise dinners at private Nubian homes and sailing and motor boat tours on the Nile.

From Aswan to Abu Simbel, there is a police convoy going daily at 4 and 11 o'clock in the morning, which starts at the obelisk in Aswan. If you want to use the convoy, be there one hour in advance. They will speed through the desert at about 130 km/h or 80 mph (or so we have been told)—with accidents occurring. **We chose not to use this convoy** and simply went to the police/military checkpoint at 10:30 in the morning. Nobody spoke English. They checked the car registration and driver's ID and off we went all alone through the desert. It is a 290-kilometre (180-mile) drive and there are petrol stations on the way. I would still fill up in Aswan, however, as not all petrol stations have electricity and fuel at the same time!

We went to Abu Simbel one day in advance as we wanted to visit the temples and **you cannot go to the Abu Simbel temples and cross the border on the same day**, because the border is only open between 9 o'clock and 2 o'clock in the afternoon.

In Abu Simbel, you can camp near the temples on the main car park near the Tourist Police building, or ask at one of the hotels.

We took a room at the **Eskaleh Nubian Ecolodge**, a Nubian-style eco-hotel with extremely helpful people, a wonderful atmosphere and great food, beer and wine. 'Eskaleh' is locally owned and very professionally run. The rooms are very clean and the entire house is beautifully decorated. Some of their food is based on home-grown products from their own farm.

Eskaleh Nubian Ecolodge

Coordinates: N22° 20.783' E031° 37.117'
Phone: +20 (0)97 340 1288
Mobile: +20 (0)122 368 0521
Email: info@eskaleh.net

Price: Rooms cost €70–€80 incl. breakfast (children under six are free of charge). They also do lunch and dinner.

The **car ferry leaves directly from Abu Simbel** (the meeting point is usually at Bank Cairo) and it takes about one hour.

From the port on the other side of Lake Nasser to the border post between Egypt and Sudan, it is a drive of about 35 km (22 miles).

The Egyptian fixer will go with you on the ferry to the border and will take care of all bureaucratic procedures together with you on the Egyptian side.

The border opens at 9:00 o'clock in the morning and they open and close the gate for each car separately.

After entering, we had to drive to customs where they wanted to scan every bag (!) and also check the car. **At borders, we always try to take control of the procedure** instead of letting others search our Land Rover. The kids stay inside the car and are allowed to watch a video on the iPad and Juliane brings the bags to the scanner while I show the officials every box and locker ('Do you want to see this?' … 'May I show you that?'). During this process, we are always friendly, but also very slow. Generally, there is only one scanner and other people are waiting, too. Which means sometimes the officials will just give up and let us drive on. They also wanted to see the boxes on the roof rack and as they were 'heavy' (they were not!), the officer had to come up with me while I showed him what was inside. For a bit of light relief, the other customs officers shook the car while he was on the roof.

After that, I insisted on being allowed to park the Land

Rover in the shade because of the kids.

After customs, both the traffic police and immigration offices had to be provided with paper work until finally, we were allowed to leave Egypt.

Our 'fixer', Kamal Muawad, did a good job and we would certainly recommend him. The only thing we had to do a lot of was waiting (we had tea with truck drivers, ate our lunch and had several conversations with passers-by while he did his job).

During our first days in Sudan, Kamal also helped us out by loaning us 2,150 Sudanese pounds, as there is no bank in Wadi Halfa (the exchange rate was 9.18 Sudanese pounds to the euro instead of the black-market rate of 11.30 in Khartoum, but certainly better than the official exchange rate which is around 7 Sudanese pounds per euro).

After you have passed the gate on the Egyptian side, you will reach the Sudanese gate after about 100 m (110 yards).

For the Sudanese side, you might need another fixer.

We chose to take Magdi Boshara.

Contact Details:
    Phone 1: +249 (0)12 173 0885
    Phone 2: +249 (0)12 226 2060
    Email: nubatia51@yahoo.com

Why? Because he offered us the cheaper price of US$420 (instead of the offer of US$500 from Mazar Mahir, who also has a good reputation on the HUBB).

Contact Details for Mazar Mahir:
    Phone: +249 (0)12 238 0740
    Mobile: +249 (0)91 107 5226

Email: <u>mazarhalfa@gmail.com</u>

On the Sudanese side, you go to the 'arrivals hall', where you have to fill in three forms with your personal details: the entry card, the document for the 'Alien Registration Department' (so you are officially registered ALIENS now!) and one document for the security police. For the 'Alien Registration Department', you will need one passport photocopy and a passport photo for each passport.

We were also placed on the central register for Khartoum, so we would not have to register elsewhere on our way through Sudan, unless we stayed longer than one month. Cameras don't seem to need to be registered anymore (do not take photos of checkpoints, any police and army buildings, post offices, bridges, powerlines etcetera!).

After an endless three hours of waiting in the arrivals hall, the car was inspected (five minutes, just a quick peep, before asking whether we had any beer) and we were free to leave.

The complete procedure at the border took us 5 hours and 20 minutes (not including ferry times and driving to the border post) and they were extremely friendly on both sides, but especially so on the Sudanese side.

The big question on the net concerning this border seems to be 'Fixer or no fixer!?' For us, on the one hand having one was very convenient—who knows how long it would have taken us without a fixer if it already took over five hours with their help? We also think that—especially in these times of very little tourism and practically no overlanders crossing this particular border—paying for the services of a fixer also helps in supporting local families. Being a fixer is not a negative or illegal profession, but a valid, licensed job using people educated by customs. From what we heard from other overlanders, this border crossing seems to be the only one where a fixer might actually be necessary.

Sudanese Visa
Visa costs: US$50 each
Fixer: US$50 paid for two adults and two kids, i.e. US$12.50 per person
Total costs: US$250/€220

Border Egypt–Sudan
Total cost Egyptian side (incl. fixer): E£1640 (€192.13). Includes all costs and ferry.
Total cost Sudanese side (incl. fixer): US$420. Includes all costs (and in our case, one night at Magdi's home, dinner and lunch and help with the SIM cards).
Total costs: US$640/€557

Crossing without the Help of a Fixer
By Sabine Hoppe and Thomas Rahn, June 2015 (www. abseitsreisen.de)

Processing at the Border Posts Wadi Halffa–Qustul

The ferry from Wadi Halfa to Aswan is no longer necessary. Since the beginning of 2015, there has been a new border that connects Halfa to Wadi via a tarmac road. On the Egyptian side, the road runs a tight 30 km (18 miles) up to the reservoir. From here, several ferries run several times a day to Abu Simbel. The crossing takes about 1.5 hours.

The border crossing from Sudan to Egypt is still a thing of mystery to many travellers, although a long ferry ride is no longer the case. It should always cost around US$500 and would not be possible without assistance, or so we had heard.

We did a lot of research online until we came across the blog of Sabine and Hans-Peter from Austria, who travelled with their two motorcycles. On www.5continents.at, they described how they made the crossing without paying the expensive assistance costs. Encouraged by this information, we also tried without assistance and would like to report our experience here.

Departing from Sudan with Border Assistance

We called someone who offered 'border assistance' and asked about the costs we should expect on the Sudanese side:

>**Customs Duty:** S£160
>**Street Tax:** S£250
>**Traffic Police:** S£140
>**Exit Stamp:** S£240
>**Cost for Border Assistance:** S£150
>**Total:** S£940 (so around €90 just for the departure from Sudan)

Using the help of the well-known 'Mazar', they paid a total amount of S£1000 (about €100). S£750 border fees plus additional S£250 for Mazar's help. Mazar did not actually charge them S£250, but he leaves it up to the traveller to decide how much they appreciate his help. They told us that all tasks were taken care of by Mazar at the border. Receipts for the expenses incurred were not offered to them.

We couldn't believe that the departure from a country could be so expensive. So we tried our luck without it.

Departing from Sudan without Border Assistance

Before we start: It **is** possible and much cheaper.

Your vehicle can be parked directly in front of the border area. A small door on the right leads to a large migration hall. An official checks the passports shortly before intake.

There are a number of counters in the migration building on the right side. Here, we were given two different forms (both in Arabic and English). An official took the passports and completed forms and put them behind another counter. The passports were then processed from there and stamped immediately. Done! There weren't any fees involved for this step.

The container-like customs building is located behind the migration building on the right side. We reached it by going straight through the fence immediately upon exiting the migration hall. The traffic police station is located in the first room on the left-hand side. Here, the following documents were photocopied: carnet of passage, driving licenses, international driving permits, vehicle insurance and both passports. The police officer at the desk retained some copies, but the rest were given back to us. There was no fee involved for the copying of these documents.

Different customs offices are located in the other containers. We presented the carnet of passage and all of our photocopies in the middle room. The officer had a think, discussed everything with a colleague and asked for Mazar, the border assistant. We had rejected Mazar's assistance. Nevertheless, the officer contacted him, but Mazar was not in the vicinity. Another man in civilian clothes showed up and took the paperwork himself.

While we waited in an air-conditioned building and got into a conversation with the officials, the Carnet de Passages was processed in the building next door. Mazar also eventually appeared and we exchanged a few words. After about 30 minutes, we received our stamped carnet.

An official led us to a further customs office. Here, we received our first bill: S£108 for customs plus S£50 for carnet processing. After we ensured that we wouldn't be charged any additional costs, we paid up and kept a printed copy of the receipt for the S£108; the S£50 is not listed on this receipt.

We returned to our vehicle and drove through the border area. The receipt for the S£108 was requested at the gate. Done!

Important Note

Traffic police fees are only incurred during entry and not during exit. An official representative of the traffic police who we met a few days earlier in Abri explained this to us. Mazar, whom we had (coincidentally?) met at the border, claimed that we had to pay this fee. However, after arguing with Mazar, the police officer at the border confirmed our point of view; that we did NOT have to pay the fee. Personally, this discrepancy in opinion alone makes the offered 'border assistance' appear very questionable.

Conclusion for Sudan

> **Time Required:** 2.5 hours
> **Total Costs:** S£158 (about €15)

Compared to S£750 (€70) in 'fees' plus an additional payment to the 'helper' for crossing with assistance. Please draw your own conclusions.

All of the officials were extremely friendly and helpful. The fee of S£108 per vehicle seemed to be obligatory, the S£50 fee for the processing done by the officials might possibly be a little corrupt. We were lucky Mazar didn't appear earlier, as it seems that he wouldn't have been any help for us; rather the opposite.

Entering Egypt with Border Assistance

According to internet myths and legends, entry into Egypt should also not be possible without full understanding of the Arabic language.

'Kamal' offers his services on the Egyptian side and many travellers rave about him. We had learned from other travellers who made the journey a few weeks earlier that it would cost about US$300 with Kamal's help, including the ferry, plus a fee of US$50 as a service fee for Kamal. This seemed to be a lot to us, so we tried on our own.

Entering Egypt without Border Assistance

Before we start, let us tell you that entry is tedious with lots of running back and forth, but it is possible without help, especially if you know a little about what to expect. Again, it is clearly cheaper without border assistance.

Important: We had organised an Egyptian visa in advance when in Khartoum. We were not sure if we could apply for visas at the border.

Before you are permitted to enter the border area, an entry fee is requested from the border control post. This is written on a large sign in front of the door which said:

> E£50 per person
> E£90 per vehicle plus an additional charge for the size of the vehicle. In our case, E£30 extra.

E£10 for weight or weighing fee. We did not understand this despite asking for clarification four times

E£5 per hour, and the assumed amount of four hours, so E£20.

Total cost for our vehicle: E£250

By the way: a camel costs E£55.

The bank on the border exchanges US dollars and euro, but not Sudanese pounds. We could exchange our remaining Sudanese money at the border café at the rate of S£10 to E£7.

A police officer checked our passport and gave us each an entry form (written in both Arabic and English).

After paying the entry fee (for each section of border control, we were given a printed receipt), we were allowed to drive our vehicle through the border gate and park on the left-hand side. Now our additional luggage had to be passed through an X-ray machine. As we didn't have any hand luggage, a customs officer came to inspect our vehicle. He opened some of the compartments, asked a few questions and continued looking around. The entire vehicle check took about ten minutes.

We followed the official into a small office on the left. Before he could process our carnet de passage, we needed a copy of the driver's passport. This copy can be made in the middle of a long building, in room number 119. Because more copies would be required in the course of this procedure, we were told we would pay photocopying costs at the end of the process.

Once he had the passport copy, we went back to the customs

office. Our visa would be valid until 23.7.15 (the day of our border crossing was 1.7.15). The official pointed out that the temporary import document could only be issued for 22 days. Because this period was too short for us, we chose to only go through immigration, hoping to get a permit to stay for 30 days.

Immigration control occurs in the first room of the long building. Here, we handed over our passports and the completed entrance forms. The passports were stamped and we were now allowed to stay in Egypt for 45 days.

Back at the customs office, we were told that the import paper could now be set up for a 30 day period and that we now had to pay the import fee of E£522.

Payments are made in a room between the customs and migrations offices. We paid and were given a receipt.

After presenting this receipt in the customs office, we received a stamp in our carnet de passage as well as a temporary import permit valid for 30 days.

We still needed Egyptian license plates. For this, you need copies of the following documents:

- Completed and stamped carnet
- Temporary import permit
- Driver's license, both front and back
- Driver's passport
- Vehicle registration, both front and back

Additionally, you will also need vehicle insurance. Our COMESA was not recognised. We did not argue about this. You can get vehicle insurance in room 117 directly next to the copy room. Insurance costs E£259 for 30 days plus a processing fee of E£20. They didn't want to give a receipt for the extra E£20, but we insisted on getting one. Because of this, the 'processing fee' was cancelled.

Now the copying office needed to be paid, and we were charged E£40. After asking, we received a discount and paid E£30.

For the license plate, we had to take all of the photocopies as well as the insurance papers to room number 48 at the back of the building complex, across from the mosque. The local officials accepted our folder stuffed with copies and began to fill out countless papers.

In the meantime, we drove our vehicle so that the chassis number could be checked. A fee of E£55 was charged for the Egyptian license plates. These were immediately paid for at the counter.

Now we needed to photocopy a little grey piece of paper. For this, you have to run to the front of the building into the copy room again, copy the paper, and go back into office number 48. We got the folder full of papers back and the license plates before being sent to the right, to room number 49, where a police officer was waiting for us.

The policeman checked our forms, checked the vehicle insurance and issued an exit paper that we would need when exiting the country.

We put the license plates on the vehicle and drove through the exit gate. Here, our passports and the license receipts were checked, and the exit form was kept. After a brief glance at the vehicle, we were allowed to enter Egypt. Done!

Conclusion for Egypt

Time required: Four hours

Costs: E£250 for the entrance, E£522 for vehicle import, E£259 for the vehicle insurance, E£55 for the license plates, E£30 for the copies. The border fees here total to E£1,116. A short ferry ride across the reservoir is added later (E£450 for small trucks).

Total cost including ferry rides: E£1,566 (about €184), instead of the US$350 (around €315) it would cost with help from Kamal.

The officials were once again friendly and spoke a little English. We never had to wait for very long and were frequently moved forward. All of the costs were supplied with a receipt. The outline of the process is lengthy, but not difficult.

In our opinion, it is completely doable on your own. With the help of somebody who knows the process, we might have saved an hour and a lot of running back and forth.

Crossing the Lake at Aswan

The ferry port to cross Lake Aswan is a 44-kilometre (28-mile) drive from the border.

During Ramadan, the ferries for Abu Simbel did not run regularly until 5 p.m. as they usually did, but only until 4 p.m. The last ferry of the day had left just as we reached the port. No problem. We could stay right in front of the harbour for the night. For an orientation point: large trucks with a trailer pay E£600 for the ferry boat. We paid E£450 for our 7.5 t vehicle.

In Egypt, clocks must be set back by an hour.

Overview of the Process
(Or 'how it might have gone faster'):

- Parked in front of the door.
- Exchanged €200 at the bank or the cafeteria.
- Paid for entry: keep the receipt.
- Filled out the entrance forms.
- Drove through the border.
- Vehicle check
- Migration, visa stamps
- Copied the driver's passport.
- Went to the customs office: carnet, visa and passport were shown; provided copies of passports. Ensured that the import was valid for 30 days.
- Paid the import charge of E£522 next door.
- Went to customs with the receipt: With this, the carnet will be stamped and the import paper handed over.
- Copies of the following were made: completed and stamped carnet, temporary import allowance, driver's license both front and back, driver's passport, vehicle registration both front and back. Take your maps with you.
- Insurance arranged in the room next to the copy machine: 30 days for E£259.
- Drove to the back of the building and parked in front of room 48.
- Handed in the copies at the desk for the license plates.
- The vehicle number was written down and many forms were issued.
- Paid E£55.

- Went to copy a small grey note and paid for the copy there.
- Went back to the license plate office, gave the photocopies. License plates were then issued and the stack of papers put into a folder.
- Handed in the stack of papers next to the office, received the exit note.
- Put on the license plates and drove to the exit gate.
- Handed in the exit note and showed the license plates' receipt.
- Done. Welcome to Egypt!
- Drink tea as often as you like between each step and start some great conversations.

This was our experience. As always, this process can change overnight or two weeks later. But this should help as a rough guide. All the officials had been lovely and we were always told where to go for the next step.

Total Conclusion

Overall, staff were friendly and helpful on both sides. It is 100% possible to cross the border without assistance. Doing it on our own cost us maybe an extra hour and some running up and down, but saved us approximately €200.

Our Recommendations

There are a few smaller hotels that allow you to camp on their grounds, but it is much more fun to camp in the wild, outside the larger cities. Simply drive off the road into the desert to a place where they cannot see you from the road and put up your tent. Completely alone in the middle of the desert—an unforgettable experience!

Wadi Halfa

Hotel
Nile Hotel

Coordinates: N21° 47.687' E31° 20.889'

Basic hotel rooms come with air conditioning and an en-suite bathroom with shower and squat toilet. You are within walking distance to town, where you can find your basic shopping needs and small restaurants. We only stayed here because we had to wait for our car to be released from Egypt, as the road hadn't yet been opened when we made the Egypt–Sudan crossing.

Dongola and Surrounding Area

Things to See and Do
Naga (or Naqa) Temple
Coordinates: N16° 16.135' E33° 16.436'

This is a ruined ancient city approximately 160 km (100 miles) north-east of Khartoum. You will need to drive off the path and into the desert. This city is really impressive, especially as you will most probably be completely alone. Further on, you will find a water well where you're likely to bump into people getting water out of the well using donkeys. Very impressive, but those people aren't used to tourists, so don't act like one (or at least not like a big, brainless one).

Swimming in the Nile

If you like, the sons of the Nubian Guesthouse will accompany you for a swim in the Nile ... as long as you pay for the taxi. The trip to the Nile is in itself a great experience, because you have to take local taxis and walk through farmland areas.

Caution: Swimming in the river where there are crocodiles is not recommended, but these children do it every day and Dries also dared. Unfortunately, women are not permitted to wear bathing suits in this country, so they just have to be happy to sit with their feet in the water.

Magasil Island

You can take a taxi from the guesthouse down to the water.

The boat is used as local transport, so you're likely to share your ride to the island with a small herd of cows.

Magasil Island is a quiet, beautiful island perfect for a peaceful walk to look at the mosques, working farms and kids at play. Be prepared to have people invite you into their home for a cup of tea. Most people do not speak a word of English, but are happy to invite you inside anyway.

Rock Paintings
Coordinates: N19° 55.834' E30° 32.006'

If you are coming from Egypt, before entering Dongola, you will pass through some small villages and on your left, you will see some massive rocks. On these rocks, you will find rock paintings. You'll have to be pretty alert, as you can easily miss them.

Camel and Donkey Skeletons
On your way from Dongola to Karima, you will see a lot of skeletons along the side of the road. These are the remains of animals who were sick, weak or too old to go on. Quite a poignant sight.

Nuri Pyramids (Karima)
Coordinates: N18° 33.800' E31° 55.003'

Plenty of tiny pyramids, no one around and completely free!

Meroe Pyramids
Coordinates: N21° 47.687' E031° 20.889'

It's S£100 per person to enter the pyramids, but you can park your car at the back so you can spend the night and enjoy watching the sun set over the pyramids.

You can also ride a camel here for S£10 pp.

Camping
Nubian Guesthouse

Unfortunately, this place is no longer operating as the owners were forced to leave. However, they're trying to come back. So, in case they do return, we find it important to include this lovely guesthouse on our list of personal favourites.

Camping: US$7 pp
Room with Fan: US$10 pp
Laundry Service: S£15
Facebook: www.facebook.com/pages/Dongola-Nubian-Guest-House/216161485079693
Email: candacanubianhouse@gmail.com

Phone: +249 (0)91 544 5337

We loved this place. It is the ideal spot to take a shower after a few days in the desert. The facility is operated by a Korean couple and their three sons, who are trying to bring back the Nubian culture to Sudan.

You can camp in the courtyard or opt for a room with a fan. There is a public kitchen and the owner will also cook for you if you so wish. Both the owner and his children are lovely.

Khartoum

Things to See and Do

Omdurman Market

This is a big market here, where you will find everything you need (and don't need). An impressive sight.

Tuti Island

You will have to take a boat to get to this island.

We used to call it 'the secret beach' as you will find a lot of young Muslims having the time of their lives here singing, dancing, playing guitar, playing in the water. Girls take off their headscarves and couples meet in secret. It's a fascinating sight.

Nile Street

All along the Nile, you will find local tea ladies. Enjoy a glass of tea and enjoy the Khartoum experience. Tea = S£1, but Nile-view tea will cost you more—up to S£2–S£3.

DON'T MISS

The huge shows of hospitality—say yes to every invitation you get and be dazzled by the local hospitality, culture and world. It would be wrong to leave Sudan without drinking tea on the Khartoum streets; it's an absolute must!

Camping

National Campsite

Price: S£60/tent

You can camp on a field in the back. Not too bad, but also not brilliant as you will be sleeping next to a mosque that loudly calls the locals to prayer at 5 a.m. And it's outside of Khartoum.

International Youth Hostel

Coordinates: N15° 35.473' E32° 32.374'
Address: House No 66, St 47, Khartoum 2, Emarat, Khartoum East (Souk Two)

You can park your car in the compound and open your tent. Nothing special, but it's in the heart of Khartoum. There is electricity in the kitchen and (very slow) Wi-Fi is available in the reception area.

DO NOT GO
Blue Nile River Campsite
Used to be a very good campsite, but don't go there now! It has become expensive and very dirty!

Ethiopia

Our Experience

Ethiopia is beautiful, but exhausting!

There is much to see, a lot of unspoiled nature, a lot of green and we found it really, really beautiful. The only downside of Ethiopia is the people. Don't get us wrong—they're nice and friendly, but SO in your face! You will lose every inch of your personal space as soon as you arrive in Ethiopia. Kids will shout 'youyouyouyouyou!' at you, and this doesn't stop till you cross the next border. Everywhere you go, kids will come to you, asking for 'plasticplasticplastic!' or 'penpenpen!'

Our advice: don't give it to them. 'Why not give them a plastic bottle?' That's what we were wondering too. It's plastic. We would throw it out anyway. But when we spoke to a guide, he explained that they don't need the plastic bottle—it's kind of a game to them to 'get something from a foreigni'. They already have 10 plastic bottles and 10 pens at home. They don't really need another, they just want it because they can get it. So he advised us not to give anything, because if you do, you just encourage them to come up to and follow the 'foreigni' all the time.

You will also discover that everything you do is a big event for them—the big 'Foreigni Show'. You don't have to do anything they've never seen before; you can just be doing the dishes or washing your clothes, or sitting around, doing nothing, and they will be hovering around like flies, staring at you. In the beginning, we thought they wanted something and asked them if they needed anything. They would just say, 'no' and remain standing in their front row seats as they watched the Foreigni Show. After a while, this got very tiring, but now we think back to those moments with big grins on our faces, remembering how Ethiopia was so, so incredibly beautiful!

General Information

Capital: Addis Ababa
Language Spoken: Amharic and English
Population: 101.4 million
Religion: Christianity (Orthodox and others), Islam, African ancient religions
Currency: Ethiopian birr

ATMs: Dashen Bank, Commercial Bank of Ethiopia and Zemen Bank

Electricity: 220V, European two-pin, Type C

Climate: Main rainy season is from June to September, with a lesser rainy season from February to April.

Time Zone: UTC +3

Country Code: +251

Shops: Little local stalls and markets

Visa

A visa is required for all nationalities except Kenyans. Visas are NOT issued at the border.

Cost: US$20 per person.

Validity: 90 days

Where to Get One:

Embassy of Ethiopia, Khartoum, Sudan

Coordinates: N15° 34.821' E32° 32.519'

Note

They will only accept USD and it's difficult to find them, so make sure you bring enough from home.

Info

The embassy is only open between 8:30 a.m. and 11:30 a.m. You can get your visa in one day, but only if you come on time, as there will be long queues.

Upon arrival at the embassy, you first need to fill out the form you get from the lady sitting outside in a tiny kiosk. This form will cost you S£1. As soon as you fill out this form, you can go inside to start queuing. You will also need two passport photos.

Travelling by Car

Carnet

A carnet is not necessary, but is recommended as they will ask for one at the border.

Car Insurance

You can only use COMESA here if you're travelling south–north, and already obtained COMESA in one of the previous countries, or if you've obtained it in Eritrea.

If you're travelling north–south, this will be the first place where you can obtain the COMESA, unless you obtained it in Eritrea. However, COMESA isn't valid in the country where you bought it, so you must buy local third-party insurance for the county in which you purchase the COMESA. More information in Chapter 4: Administration.

The first insurance company you will find will probably be in Gondar. There are three insurance companies on the main street in Gondar, but only one issues the COMESA.

This insurance company is called 'UNIC ETHIOPIA— The United Insurance Company', but unfortunately and confusingly, this isn't written on the building, so you will have to look around. Alternatively, some insurance companies in Addis Ababa will issue the COMESA.

Road Conditions

The main roads, namely roads leading to Addis Ababa and Gondar, are in good condition. Other routes are often really terrible gravel roads, where it will take a whole day of driving to travel 300 kilometres (185 miles). But they are eager to build new roads in Ethiopia, which is mostly being done by Chinese companies. So by the time you go, the roads will probably have been improved.

Police

We didn't come across many police when we were travelling through Ethiopia, certainly a lot less than in other countries.

Fuel

No problems getting fuel; both diesel and petrol are available.

Car Help

The Motor & Engineering Company of Ethiopia Limited S.C.

> **Address:** Qelebet Menged, Addis Ababa
> **Phone:** +251 (0)11 663 4814
> **Website:** moencoethiopia.com

Note

Be aware of stone-throwing children on the road! It's a habit they learn from their parents, bigger brothers, uncles, aunties, etc. who throw stones at animals to get them to move and throw stones at kids when they're being naughty. In general, the kids are just bored and like to throw stones at things, especially big, shiny cars. Tip: as soon as you see a kid, start waving at them. They will wave back at you and drop their stones. This worked 99% of the time and only once did we have rocks thrown at us.

Crossing the Border

Sudan–Ethiopia

Border Used

Metema

There aren't many options; this is the primary route.

Note

Make sure you arrive on time, as Sudanese customs have lunch from 11 a.m. to 1 p.m. while Ethiopian customs have theirs between 1 p.m. and 3 p.m.! We arrived at 10:50 a.m. and were finally moved on at 3:30 p.m.! Because of this, we had to drive to the first town we could find in the dark, which we don't recommend.

Formalities

Sudanese Side

- They write your name down.
- You fill out an exit form.
- You get an exit stamp for your passport.
- You get an exit stamp for your carnet.

Ethiopian Side

- They write your name down.
- You fill out an entry form.
- You get an entry stamp for your passport.
- You get an entry stamp for your carnet.

Note

On the Ethiopian side, we got the feeling they were going through our vehicle more out of curiosity than for official requirements.

Our Recommendations

There are a lot of hotels, but no campsites at all. However, you are often given permission to camp on the hotel compounds/backyards of hotels if you ask them. Prices are negotiable and they will often let you use the facilities (shower and toilet) if you ask.

Gondar

Things to See

Royal Enclosure

The Royal Enclosure is within walking distance from Belegeze Pension and costs 100 birr pp to enter.

A sign states that you also have to pay for your camera, but no-one asked us to pay for ours.

Camping

Belegeze Pension

Coordinates: N12° 36.638' E37° 28.316'
Price: 81 birr for two

This is a compound with lots of little rooms dotted about. They will allow you to park your car inside the compound. It's a small area, fitting approximately three vehicles. There is always someone on-site to keep an eye on your car. They have power in the rooms; we didn't use any, but I think they will let you use a socket if you ask.

Restaurant

Opposite the pension is a very good restaurant that is not expensive.

Not too far from the pension is the '4 Sisters'. The food is good, but more expensive as it's very touristy here. While you eat, local dancers will entertain you. It's nice to see, but we didn't appreciate being part of a tourist attraction.

Debark

This town contains the head office where you will start your trip to the Simien Mountains. It's perfectly possible to arrange everything yourself, but we decided to use a tour company that we had booked in Gondar (see below). You might be able to leave your car here if you go on a walking tour, but we decided to take ours.

Things to Do
Simien Mountain

Wonderful! We just loved it! We used a tour operator in Gondar that pre-booked everything for us.

> **Tour Operator:** Simien Mountain Trekking PLC, Baboon Trekking and Tour
> **Where to Find It:** Atse Bekaffa Hotel.
> **Phone:** +251 (0)91 877 1714

We paid US$50 pp for three days in a group of six people. The price is dependent on the type of trip and the number in your group. This trip is all-inclusive (meals, tents, guides, scouts, cooks). You can also try to arrange a trip yourself in Debark. This might end up being a little bit cheaper.

You will need a guide and a scout to walk through the Simien mountains, and you can also opt for a cook and mules. Our tour included a cook and mules and we were so happy they came along. The mules carried our big backpack, meaning we only had to worry about our small daypacks. The mules don't walk with you; they take a shortcut. We should also add that this tour operator took very good care of their mules;

they avoid overloading the mules by weighing the items on primitive scales before packing them onto the mules' backs. We were surprised to see this and so relieved for the mules' sakes.

The Simien mountain range is very high and the altitude will get to you from the first day. You will be happy when you get to the top, but you will be exhausted! As soon as we arrived, the cook made us hot tea and popcorn and, to our surprise, our tents had already been set up! The food was delicious—we thought we would get simple fare like pasta or rice, but we had the most wonderful meals on the trek like French fries, fresh meat and even fruit salad! These mountaintop camps can get very windy and, when we saw other hikers struggling to set up their tents and cook in gale force winds, we were happy we had taken the 'luxury' option.

If you're planning to drive and leave your vehicle at the first stop, make sure you hire a guard. We didn't do this and had some things stolen out of the car (a phone and a hairband). Even today, we're not sure if it was an outsider or a member of our group, as the car was locked when we found it. But we must also mention that our tour operator reimbursed us for the items that had been stolen.

Camping
Giant Lobelia Hotel

Coordinates: N13° 09.308' E37° 53.848'
Price: 150 birr (two persons, one car)

We stayed here after a three-day trip in the Simien Mountains, as we wanted to continue to Aksum the following day. They don't have a camping site, but we were allowed to stay in the backyard and use the staff facilities. Make sure to ask for a shower before you pay! They will normally let you use one in one of the empty rooms.

Aksum

If you're driving between Gondar and Aksum, make sure you leave on time as it took us 10 hours to cover 150 km (90 miles)! The road is extremely bad. They are improving it, but sometimes you have to wait for the bulldozers to clear the road before you can continue on your way. This was back in 2013, so the road might (perhaps) be better.

Things to Do
The Ark of the Covenant

We were in Aksum in April and were lucky enough to see a spectacular event: the tabot (a replica of the Ark of Covenant) brought out of the Holy of Holies. We had to get up at 4.30 in the morning. It was pitch black in the streets and all the locals came out of their houses dressed in white gowns and carrying candles. For the next two hours, they walked and prayed. It's quite a difficult scenario to describe, but was one of our most wondrous experiences. Have a look on our website to read the full story and look at our pictures of this incredible event.

It's not easy to find time and date information for the next procession; it will involve a lot of work using Google.

We were told that Timkat (the Ethiopian Orthodox celebration of Epiphany) is also something really worth seeing. It is held on the 19th of January each year (or on the 20th in leap years).

Camping
Atse Kaleb Hotel

Coordinates: N14° 07.371' E38° 43.373'
Price: 300 birr

They have a few rooms and you can park your car in the beer garden. The garden is quite big and not very busy, so people won't be sitting right next to your tent. There is power available inside the restaurant.

Eating
Ramish Hotel

The meals are a bit more expensive, but worth the extra cost. We were travelling during one of several Ethiopian Orthodox Church fasting periods (no meat or dairy) and this was the only restaurant that could offer us a bit of meat, which is why we went.

You can camp here and they have a swimming pool.

Adrigat

Pass through here when going from Aksum to Mekele if you want to see the churches cut into the rock.

Things to Do

Rock Churches of Tigray

You will see many churches en route. Keep in mind that you will have to pay 150 birr pp for each church! Most of them are just square concrete blocks cut into in the rocks, so choose the right one(s)!

Mekele

Things to Do

Danakil Depression

Even after completing our journey, when people ask us what the most remarkable thing was that we saw during our trip, we still say the Danakil Depression (and the gorillas). Seeing a live volcano—scorching lava bubbling up from the centre of the earth in a sulphurous other-worldly landscape—is so surreal. We can tell you about it and show you pictures, but it's nothing like experiencing it for real. Utterly unbelievable!

We researched a number of companies before we went to see the volcano and the cheapest one we could find was Ethio Travel & Tours (ETT). We joined a group of seven travellers, but used our own car. You need to make sure that the undercarriage of your vehicle is high enough from the ground, as you will be driving over some high rocks on the final day, but as you're driving through Africa, we assume this won't be a problem.

At the time of writing, the website quoted US$600 pp for the same package as the one we had bought; however, as this is Ethiopia, you can haggle. The price will of course depend on the size of the group. We paid US$250 pp when we made the trip (2013), but by now it might be more expensive.

Just send ETT an email and negotiate a price. It's quite a lot of money, but *so* worth it!

> **Duration:** Four days from Mekele to Mekele
> **Price:** US$250 pp with own car (2013 price)

This price includes:

- All entrance fees and licenses as per the programme
- Accommodation in Afar village and all meals for the duration of the tour (beds are made from ropes and out in the open)
- Non-alcoholic beverages with meals as per the programme and plenty of 1.5 litre bottles of water for the trip (but they are boiling hot!)
- Local guide service for the Afar region as per the programme
- Scout and police service in Afar Region as per the programme
- Experienced cook for the duration of the tour as per the programme
- Government taxes—VAT

For the duration of the trip, we were financially responsible for all meals, entrance fees, accommodation, security and an extra vehicle.

If you want to drive your own vehicle, you will need permission to enter with your car. This costs US$50 and the agency will happily arrange it for you.

Booking

You can send them an email beforehand at ethiopiatravel@ gmail.com to discuss the price, or you can drop by their office. They are located behind the Atse Yohannes Hotel (see coordinates above).

Itinerary
www.ethiotravelandtours.com

Day 1: Mekele–Hamed Ela, Drive to Hamed Ela via Berhale.

The Danakil Depression can be said to begin here. It is one of the most inhospitable regions of the world, but is nonetheless spectacular, full of eye-catching colours in the form of sulphur springs. The desert has several points lying more than 100 metres (328 ft) below sea level. You pass through the small town of Berhale, where the camel caravans stop before they proceed to the northern highlands. En route, you see many long camel caravans coming to the salt mine and others going out of the Danakil with their salt-laden camels. It's a three-to-four-hour drive to Camp Hamed Ela.

Day 2: Hamed Ela–Dodom

Start early to drive to Dodom (at the base of Mt Erta Ale). Leave after an early breakfast, possibly at 6:30 a.m. This may be one of the worst roads in the world. The 80-kilometre (50-mile) trip may take about six hrs, and passes through changing landscapes of solidified lava, rock, sand and the occasional palm-lined oasis. After you pass several small hamlets scattered here and there in this desert land, Dodom is about 17 km (10 miles) from Erta Ale. Early dinner is around 5 p.m., and the trek up to Erta Ale's summit starts at 8:00 p.m.

The trek takes about three hours. Camels transport all the camping materials (sleeping materials like light mattresses and mats) and some food (and water) to the rim of the volcano, where we spent the night watching the dramatic action of the boiling lava. Erta Ale ranks as one of the most alluring and physically challenging natural attractions anywhere in Ethiopia. It is a shield volcano with a base diameter of 30 km (18 miles) and the caldera at its summit covers a square kilometre (247 acres) in area. It is 613 metres (2,011 ft) high and contains the world's only permanent lava lake, which is notable for being the longest-existing lava lake, present since the early years of the twentieth century.

Overnight at the top of the mountain.

Day 3: Descend from Erta Ale around 9 a.m. Dodom–Hamed Ela.

Leave for Dodom after an early breakfast, if possible at 7:00 a.m. You will reach the camp at 10:30 a.m. at the latest, with a bit of time to relax. After a drive, reach Hamead Ela, a better village with a total population about 500 people. Overnight camping at Hamed Ela.

Day 4: Morning Tour Drive to Ragad (Asebo), where the locals mine salt.

See the activity of breaking the salt from the ground, cutting it into rectangular pieces and loading the pieces onto camels.

Excursion to Dallol, which is 116 metres (380 ft) below sea level, making it one of the lowest places in the world.

See the colourful salt mining, visit Lake Assal, follow up camel caravans and walk with the Afar people.

Drive back to Hamed Ela and proceed to Mekele.

Camping
Hohole Hotel

> **Coordinates:** N14° 16.573' E39° 27.452'
> **Price:** We were allowed to stay for free as it was the first time they had had an overlander visit. We just parked in the tiny courtyard among the sheep.

This isn't a campsite, but we couldn't find anything else and the owner was extremely friendly, since it was the first time they had an overlander to stay.

Ok, there were two sheep next to our car and it wasn't much of a campsite, but we got to stay there for free.

If we might suggest anything from the menu, try 'Dabo frefre', bread cooked with tomatoes and onion. Delicious!

Hotel
Atse Yohannes Hotel

Coordinates: N13° 29.344' E39° 28.396'
Address: Selam Street, Mekele, Ethiopia

We stayed in a room as we had just come back from Danakil and wanted a proper shower, but you might be able to 'camp' in their car park.

Lalibela

Camping
Bena Baba

Coordinates: N12° 02.561' E39° 02.228'
Price: Free
Email: info@benabeba.com
Phone: +251 (0)92 234 5122

This is a lovely restaurant built on a mountain, so you have a wonderful view during breakfast! The lady is Irish and she's planning to make a little campsite next to the restaurant, but at the moment there is nothing and you can stay there for free! Food is a bit more expensive, but it is really good. Power is available in the restaurant.

Gorgora

Things to Do

Tim and Kim Village is right on Lake Tana, so have a swim or take a little boat ride, but beware the hippos. Check with the campsite first!

Camping

Tim & Kim Village

Coordinates: N12° 13.740' E37° 17.930'
Price: 95 birr pp
Phone 1: +251 (0)92 033 6671
Phone 2: +251 (0)91 830 0425
Website: www.timkimvillage.com
Email: info@timkimvillage.nl, timandkimvillage@yahoo.com

This campsite is run by a woman from the Netherlands. Travelling through Ethiopia is very exhausting, as everyone is always begging and staring, and you never seem to have enough personal space or time.

When we drove to this campsite, a lot of kids were following us and shouting (the usual stuff in Ethiopia), but as soon as we drove through the gates, it was an oasis of peace! Only campers are allowed past the gate and it was quiet and peaceful—just what we needed!

Bahir Dar

Things to Do
Boat Trips to the Island Monasteries

They do boat trips to the monasteries on the islands, but we thought it was a waste of money. The monastery we visited was really small and our guide only had enough English and knowledge to tell us, 'the monastery is really old', 'this Jesus', 'this Maria!' They also said we would definitely see hippos, but we didn't. Wasn't worth the money to us.

Camping
Gion Hotel

Unfortunately, this hotel is closed at the time of writing.

Coordinates: N11° 35.857' E37° 23.147'

Nice hotel which has a space in the back where you can park your car and stay for the night. They also have a lovely beer garden.

Addis Ababa

DON'T MISS
Laundry

If you've got white clothes with you, in Ethiopia they sell a soap that makes even the dirtiest shirt white again! Not sure what's in it, but it works. You can find this soap in the local markets; it's a white piece of soap with a design stamped into it. Ours had a peacock.

Food

Try shiro (breakfast) in a local restaurant, then get some of your own from the market. You buy it as a red powder and you only need water to prepare it. We've used it throughout our trip.

Camping
Wim's Holland House

Wim's Holland House is located in the centre of Addis Ababa. Drive to La Gare (bus station). When you are facing the railway station, turn left onto a small dirt road. Drive straight on and take the second street to the left. After 10 metres, you will find Wim's Holland House on the right-hand side.

> **Coordinates:** N09° 00.589' E03°45.325'
> **Price:** Small car: €5, big car: €7, tent: €3
> **Internet:** 20 birr/30 minutes. This is a dongle that you have to plug into your laptop.
> **Phone:** +251 (0)91 160 8088
> **Phone (Rahel):** +251 (0)91 188 7770
> **Email:** wimshollandhouse@gmail.com

The campsite is a tiny grass area opposite the restaurant. There is a toilet and a big sink to wash your clothes in, if you want to. In the restaurant, you can find some real Dutch food and drink such as 'bitterballen' and Heineken! They also have a maintenance pit in the garden, which is ideal if you need to check underneath your vehicle or fix something! They have cold showers on the camping ground and hot showers in the rooms. Power points are available in the restaurant.

Kenya

Our Experience

We loved Kenya. This was the first country where we got to see 'real' wildlife and we will never forget how excited we were about spotting our first zebra, how amazed we were at the beauty of a giraffe in its natural habitat and how blown away we were when an elephant passed in front of our car.

We took the route via Lake Turkana and that was a big adventure in itself; 10 days in the middle of nowhere. No water, no food, no shade ... and our car broke down. It was crazy and scary, but we would do it again in an instant.

Kenya is a country where tourism is up and coming, so expect better English ... and of course, more tourists.

But there are more than enough lovely spots where you can take your vehicle to escape the tourists. Be prepared to be amazed!

General Information

Capital: Nairobi

Language Spoken: English and Swahili

Population: 47 million

Religion: Protestant 45%, Roman Catholic 33%, Muslim 10%, indigenous beliefs 10%, other 2%. Note: a large majority of Kenyans are Christian, but estimates for the percentage of the population that adheres to Islam or indigenous beliefs vary widely.

Currency: Kenyan shilling (KES)

ATMs: Equity, Barclays and KCB

Electricity: 240V, Type G

Climate: January to March is warm and dry; March to June is the rainy season; June to October is cool and dry; November to December is a rainy season.

Time Zone: UTC +3

Country Code: +254

Shops: In Nairobi, you will find the first big supermarket where prices are clearly labelled and everyone pays the same price. Heaven! But there are still markets and little shops, which we know need your support.

Visa
Coming from Ethiopia
Where to Get One

As we were driving into Kenya via Lake Turkana, there was no border, so we picked up our visas in the Kenyan Embassy in Addis Ababa, Ethiopia.

Coordinates: N09° 01.945' E038° 46.994'
Address: High 16 Kebelle 01,
Addis Ababa, Ethiopia
Phone: +251(0)11 661 0033

Requirements

- Your passport
- US$50
- One picture
- One copy of your passport

The embassy is open from 9:30 a.m.–12:30 p.m. and it takes 48 hours before your visa is ready, so it's a good idea to come early in the morning.

Duration: 90 days
Processing: 48 hours

Coming from Uganda

Cost: US$50
Duration: 90 days
Where to Get One: At the border

East African Visa
www.migration.gov.rw/index.php?id=233

Since 2014, you can get an Eastern African visa, which allows you to travel between Uganda, Kenya and Rwanda with the same multiple entry visa.

> **Cost:** US$100
> **Validity:** 90 days
> **Where to Get One:** You have to apply for the visa at the border of the country you enter first.

Note

There are rumours saying that you have to apply at an embassy or consulate in your home country, but many travellers have been able to simply obtain the visa at the border without any issues.

If you're planning to visit Rwanda first, you can apply online (which, at the moment of writing, is not possible for Kenya or Uganda). Within three days, you will get a confirmation email that you will need to show at the Rwandan border.

We have heard mixed information; some people were able to get one immediately at the Rwandan border, others had to have the email confirmation.

Travelling by Car

Carnet

You will need a carnet.

If you come into Kenya via Lake Turkana, there are a few things you need to do when actually arriving in Nairobi, as there are no customs when you cross the border.

- You will have to pass by immigration and register your arrival. You do this at Nyayo House in the centre of Nairobi (the big yellowish building at Posta St).
- You have to pass through customs to get your carnet stamped and pay road tax. This is done at Times Tower (also known as New Central Bank Tower), a tall grey building within walking distance (10 min.) of Nyayo house.

It's quite easily done; the only problem is finding a parking spot.

Car Insurance
COMESA

Road Conditions
In Kenya, they drive on the left. Generally speaking, the roads are not in very good condition. Even tarmac roads are badly maintained and driving is difficult due to deep holes. We recommend driving very carefully on the tarmac, as suddenly—out of nowhere—big potholes will appear. There are also very dangerous speed bumps everywhere. Gravel roads are often in a terrible condition and it takes a long time to travel 100 kilometres (60 miles).

Police
Traffic police in Kenya wear dark blue trousers or skirts and a light blue shirt. Remember, always remain polite and calm. We didn't have any major problems with them, apart from the occasional check of our driving licenses.

Fuel
No problems getting fuel: diesel and petrol are available.

Note

Be careful! The petrol attendants know every trick in the book!

Road Tax

KES 3,600 (approx. US$40) for 30 days.

Car Help

CMC (Commercial Motor Spares)

Coordinates: S01° 18.250' E036° 49.941'
Address: 13 Dunga Rd/10 Bandan Rd
Phone 1: +254 (0)20 552 545
Phone 2: +254 (0)20 552 586
Phone 3: +254 (0)20 552 458
Email: info@cms.co.ke
Note: Here you can find genuine brand parts—we got parts for our Toyota here.

Nairobi Toyota, Uhuru highway/Lusaka Road

Address: Uhuru Highway/Lusaka Road
Phone: +254 (0)20 696 7000
Mobile: +254 (0)71 902 9000
Email: enquiries@toyotakenya.com

RMA Motors (Kenya) Limited

Address: Enterprise Road, off Mombasa Road, Opposite Jomo Kenyatta Foundation
Phone 1: +254 (0)71 411 0110
Phone 2: +254 (0)73 019 1000
Phone 3: +254 (0)73 019 0000
Email: enquiries@landroverkenya.com
Note: Official Landrover dealership

Car Mechanic

Joe is the manager of a mechanic shop just outside the centre of Nairobi. He speaks excellent English and helped us out when we were in big trouble with our car. We can only give you the coordinates of the workplace. Check it out if you're in trouble!

Coordinates: S01° 19.149' E036° 50.799'

Crossing the Border

Kenya–Uganda

Border:
We crossed over in Busia, which took us 1 hr 45 min.

Formalities

Ugandan Side
- Get a stamp in the carnet.
- Fill out the departure form.
- Fingerprints and picture.
- Get a stamp in your passport.

Kenyan Side
- Get a stamp in the carnet.
- Fill out the entry form.
- Visa stamp: US$50.

Ethiopia–Kenya

You can cross into Ethiopia via different routes. We chose to cross via Lake Turkana and, for this reason, we can (obviously) only relate our personal experiences of this crossing.

Lake Turkana

The route along Lake Turkana was one of the highlights of our trip. It's a very remote area, without easy access to supplies. You will be without water, fuel and shade for days, so we recommend teaming up to do this trip. Make sure you check the weather forecast before you start planning, as there will be a few riverbed crossings. We went in June and everything was as dry as it could be.

Keep in mind that we did this route in 2013, so things might have changed!

The time indication we give below is the actual driving time (breaks not included).

Day 1: JINKA–TUMI
Distance: 90 km (55 miles), Time: 2 hrs 30 min.
We drove 20 km (12 miles) on tarmac before hitting gravel, and that was the last tarmac we saw for days.

Camping: Mango Campsite

Coordinates: N04° 58.570' E036° 30.945'

This is a tiny place where you can open up your tent between the trees. The people there are friendly and at night, you might see some strange bushbaby-like animals (we had no idea what they were). They have a water pump here and this is the last time you can fill up on water. It's not drinkable.

If you're travelling in the right season, you might be able to watch the 'bull jumping', an Ethiopian traditional coming-of-age ceremony.

DAY 2: TUMI–BUSHCAMP

Distance: 154 km (96 miles), Time: 3 hrs 10 min.

On your way, you have to stop at the immigration office in Omorate to get 'OUT' stamps in both your visas and carnet.

Omorate Immigration:
Coordinates: N04° 48.336' E036° 03.066'

Note

We had a problem. In our carnet, they had filled in the wrong 'out' city, so make sure you double check when entering Ethiopia. Otherwise, just be very polite, ask about their family and put on your sweetest smile.

This is also the last town where you can purchase supplies for a while, or change your money.

From Omorate to the Kenyan border should only take 30 minutes, but it is a very bad road.

There is also nothing to see there; you will only see the border as indicated by your navigator.

You will pass through a tiny settlement called 'Ileret' and apparently, you have to write down your details here in an 'Incident Book'. However, when we passed by, all we found was an empty building ...

When you're in Nairobi and go to the immigration to state your arrival, they may ask where you entered Kenya and they may ask for proof which you should have received at Ileret. We didn't have this, but didn't encounter any problems because of it.

At the end of day 2, we slept in the bush!

Day 3: BUSHCAMP–SIBILOI NATIONAL PARK

Distance: 114 km (70 miles), Time: 5 hrs

The journey here starts with a relatively gentle sandy road, where you can reach comfortable speeds of 30–40 km/h (18–25 mph) until it changes into a gravel road, bringing your speed to around 30 km/h (18 mph).

On your way, you will also pass a few dry river beds (time to make use of your 4WD!), as well as pass a little oasis with palm trees and water in the middle of the desert—well worth a stop, we think.

We tried to drive around Sibiloi National Park to avoid the fees, but the borders had recently been changed, so when we tried to leave, we couldn't find a way out. We ended up paying US$20 per person.

Tonight, we slept in the bush!

Day 4: BUSHCAMP–LOIANGOLANI

Distance: 120 km (74 miles), Time: 3 h 30 min.

The road changes a lot. On some stretches, you can drive between 30 and 50 km/h (18–30 mph), with a few steep riverbeds on the way.

Today, you will get your first views of the beautiful Lake Turkana.

Camping: Palm Shade Camp

Coordinates: N02° 75.630' E36° 72.120'
Price: 500 KES pp

Note

This is the first 'real' camp with a shower, shade and beer! There are a few others scattered around, but we found this to be the best one. They have a hot (!) shower (solar charged, so make sure you get in first).

Day 5: LOIYANGALANI
Distance: 0 km, Time: 0 hrs

We stayed at the campground for an extra day so we could rest and check over our vehicles.

Day 6: LOIYANGALANI–SOUTH HORR
Distance: 89 km (55 miles), Time: 3 hrs 50 min.

On this stretch, the road is very bad. You will only manage speeds of around 25–30 km/h (15–18 mph).

Camping: Samburu Sport Centre Guesthouse

> **Coordinates:** N36° 92.420' E02° 10.670'
> **Price:** 500 KES pp

Note

If you would like something to drink, one of the guys will jump on his bike and cycle into to town to get you something.

The drink will be warm, though.

Day 7: SOUTH HORR–MARALAL
Distance: 144 km (89 miles), Time: 5 hrs 10 min.

Maralal is the first town where you will find shops and an ATM again.

Camping: Safari Lodge

Coordinates: N36° 71.100' E01° 05.900'
Price: Camping: 500 KES pp

Note
Has a nice grass field a bit further from the lodge. The zebras will come and join you!

We had access to the lodge, so we could take a nice, hot shower.

They have a pretty little restaurant/bar from where you can watch the zebras. You can find power points in the bar/restaurant or in the lodge.

Day 8: MARALAL
Distance: 0 km, Time: 0 hrs
We had another rest day today.

Day 9: MARALAL–THOMPSON'S FALLS
Distance: 159 km (98 miles), Time: 5 hrs 30 min.
Very bad road!

We asked the locals how long it would take us and they said, 'usually three hours, but with your car, two'.

It took us five hours!

Over the last 42 km (25 miles), almost invisible bumps suddenly appear in the road, so watch out.

Camping: Thompson Falls Lodge

Price: Camping 800 KES pp

Address: Thomson's Falls Lodge is located in the South East of Nyahururu Town, about 180 kilometres (112 miles) from Nairobi.

Note

Has a nice grass field a bit behind the building, where you can camp. You can walk to the falls. Very pretty, big falls—worth a stop!

Day 10. THOMPSON'S FALLS–NAIROBI
Distance: 204 km (127 miles), Time: 3 hrs 45 min.

Again, there are those dangerous bumps on the way which are not easy to see, so don't drive too fast and keep an eye out for them.

Traffic in Nairobi is very busy, try to avoid driving during daylight hours in the week as there is so much traffic you will find it hard to even get moving. Saturday is quieter, but Sunday is the best time to drive.

Our Recommendations

There are a lot of hotels and campsites along the coast. You are also often allowed to camp on hotel grounds if you ask nicely, especially in more rural areas. There are a lot of campsites in Kenya compared to other countries, with varying standards.

Lake Naivasha

Camping
Fisherman's Camp

Coordinates: S00° 49.548' E036° 20.950'
Price: 600 KES per person per night, 300 KES per child (3–12 years).
Address: Naivasha Town Fisherman's Camp, Southlake Matatu
Phone: +254 (0)72 687 0590
Email: fishermanscamp@gmail.com
Website: www.fishermanscamp.com
Facebook: www.facebook.com/pages/Fishermans-Camp-Lake-Naivasha-Kenya/148423271889207

This is a lovely spot! A very nice and quiet place with one of the best hot(!) showers we had on our trip.

You can camp between the trees, close to the lake, and hear the rhinos at night.

Don't confuse it with Fisher Camp!

Fisher Camp is also a nice spot, but it's more expensive and not on the lake.

Kisumu

Camping
Lakewood Hotel

> **Coordinates:** S00° 07.972' E034° 44.736'
> **Price:** 500 KES
> **Address:** Off Dunga Road, Dunga Beach Kisumu City
> **Email:** lakewoodhotel1@gmail.com, admin@lakewoodhotel.co.ke
> **Facebook:** www.facebook.com/pages/Lakewood-Hotel-Kisumu/1482571172021380

If it's too busy at the Kenya Wildlife Club, this is a good alternative as all the other places in the area are very expensive. This place doesn't really have a garden to camp in, but it's the only reasonably priced place we could find in the area when we were here the first time. The last five minutes is on a very bad road and it looks as you're driving out of town, but don't give up. We were allowed to stay in front of the hotel in their courtyard and, as there was no one else in the hotel, it was really nice. The staff was also very friendly. It was raining very heavily and they offered to let us stay in a room for the same price as the amount we were paying to stay in the tent. They serve lovely fresh tilapia in the restaurant and there are power points you can use in the restaurant, too.

Kenya Wildlife Club

Price: 500 KES pp
Phone: +254 (0)72 465 6667
Address: Langata road, situated behind the sunset Hotel next to Jaramogi Oginga Odinga's home.
Website: www.wildlifeclubsofkenya.org
Email: info@wildlifeclubsofkenya.org

There are a few bandas (huts) here, in a nice area with trees. We were able to park our car between the bandas. When we were there, all the bandas were empty. We're not sure if all the bandas are ever occupied, but even so, it's a nice place to stay. There is a hot shower. They don't have a bar or a restaurant, but one of the employees was absolutely lovely and went to the nearby shop to get us some pop.

Tsavo East National Park

We didn't camp in the park itself, but just outside its borders.

Camping
Tsavo Campsite

Coordinates: S03° 22.081' E038°35.233'

Price: 500 KES pp

Nice little campsite just outside the park. It looks like they're just starting up and you can see that they are doing their best. The guy there was very friendly. Unfortunately, the shower is cold, but we were the only people there, so we had no reason to complain. No bar or restaurant.

Red Elephant Lodge

> **Coordinates:** S03° 22.284' E038° 35.644'
> **Price:** 950 KES pp
> **Address:** Tsavo East National Park Road, Kenya
> **Phone:** +254 (0)72 711 2175
> **Email:** office@red-elephant-lodge.com
> **Website:** www.red-elephant-lodge.com

This is a bit further than Tsavo Lodge. They were supposed to have a hot shower, but as there was no electricity, there was no hot shower. Since it was double the price, we ended up returning to the Tsavo campsite. The Red Elephant does have a restaurant and a bar.

DON'T GO:
Tsavo Lodge
> **Coordinates:** S03° 22.284' E038° 35.644'

They told us they had a campsite, but it was actually on the parking lot in front of the building. We didn't stay because of the high price they were asking for such a badly located campsite.

Watamu

Camping
Ocean's Sport

Coordinates: S03° 21.632' E040° 00.438'
Price: 800 KES pp
Address: Mida Creek Road, Watamu 80208, Kenya
Phone: +254 (0)72 438 9732
Email: reservations@oceansports.net
Website: www.oceansports.net
Facebook: www.facebook.com/oceansportskenya

This is a really nice place, featuring a beautiful white private beach, with a nice bar and restaurant overlooking it. They also have a swimming pool with comfortable beach chairs and towels.

Unfortunately, the campsite was a bit run-down so we tried to get the price lowered, but the manager—the only one allowed to change the price—was on holiday, so the receptionist couldn't help us. As we were there out of season, we had the place to ourselves, so we ended up just paying the full price.

The shower is cold, but we were offered a room where we could use a hot shower. There's free Wi-Fi.

As it's a 'sport lodge', they have a sport going on like soccer, beach volleyball, hockey, etc. every evening. They also rent out bikes and you can go on snorkel or scuba diving tours.

Mombasa

When you cross Mombasa from north to south (and the other way round), you have to take a ferry.

It's very easy. The queue is not that long and it only takes 10 minutes to cross.

Price: 180 KES/car

DON'T MISS
Masai Mara National Reserve

We visited Masai Mara and it was unforgettable!

The only reason we went was because we won a two-night stay in one of the park lodges (lucky us).

The entrance fee is quite high (US$80 pp/24 hrs and 400 KES/car) due to its popularity with the tourists, but you're allowed to drive alone and don't need a guide or guard to accompany you like you do in some other parks.

The best time to visit the park is in the morning and the evening, but you're only allowed to drive inside after sunrise and before sunset if you're not staying in the park.

If you're not planning on staying inside the park (it *is* expensive), there are campsites outside the gates that range from US$10 to US$25 per person per night. (Oldarpoi Mara camp is US$10 per person per night.)

Enter the park in the late afternoon, as between midday and early afternoon, it's simply too hot and you won't see any animals. You can leave the park before sunset, camp just outside the gates, then wake up early and be ready to enter at the gate as soon as the sun rises.

As your ticket is valid for a full 24 hours, there's no need to purchase another ticket.

Snorkelling

Along the coast, there are a lot of beautiful places to snorkel, so bring your own snorkelling equipment!

David Sheldrick Trust
www.sheldrickwildlifetrust.org

Located in Nairobi, this is a facility where orphaned elephants are reared and prepared to be released back into the wild. Wonderful to watch the babies and keepers—and it's a good cause, too. Don't go on weekends, as it can get horribly crowded.

Camping
Twiga Lodge

Coordinates: S4° 14.487' E39° 36.138'
Price: 400 KES pp
Address: Tiwi Beach, Mombasa, Kenya
Phone: +254 (0)72 157 7614
Facebook: www.facebook.com/pages/Twiga-Lodge
/123775657718356?rf=1515891765326550

This is one of the most amazing places we've ever camped in! Twiga Lodge is on a stunning white beach and you literally camp on the sands! Park between the palm trees and wake up to a crystal clear blue sea—this is one of the most beautiful campsites we've stayed at during our entire trip.

The camping manager, 'Eddie', has a great sense of humour and is very nice.

You can buy fruit, vegetables and fish on the beach from local men who makes their rounds there and if you ask Eddie, he can provide you with bread.

It was such a gorgeous spot that we stayed until we ran out of cash. There is a restaurant/bar where you can have a limited range of food and drink as well as use the power points.

There are a few Beach Boys, but Eddie keeps a good eye on them. When we were there, it was off-season and we bought some quality wood carvings for a very low price.

There is also a nice place to snorkel nearby, but you need to take a guide with you so you don't get hassled. Eddie will point you towards an honest guide. There are two small areas where you can snorkel and we paid 500 KES for the two of us to snorkel in both places.

Uganda

Our Experience

We had a long stopover during our trip to Uganda and worked there. Because of this, we have a totally different view of this country. But the parts we did get to see were absolutely beautiful!

They call Uganda 'the pearl of Africa' and we think that's a fitting reference. A lot of greenery and, let's not forget, gorillas. The gorillas were (and probably still are) amazing! Uganda isn't as much of a tourist trap as Kenya, which means that there are still lots of unspoiled areas to discover.

Uganda has many beautiful national parks (which we didn't get to see) such as Murchison Falls and the Queen Elizabeth National Park. Keep in mind that it can be very pricy to take a foreign registered vehicle into the national parks (around US$150/car).

But there are so many other beautiful and fun things to do: rafting on the Nile, gorilla trekking ... both of these are a must!

Also try eating a 'Rolex'—an omelette wrapped in a chapatti. GREAT street food!

Working in Uganda

We worked in Uganda, and let's just say it was ... an experience ...

When you work in a foreign country, together with local people, it's only natural that you will see another side to both that country and its people.

In Uganda, we saw how people treated each other; we saw how white behaved towards black and how black behaved towards white. The experience was unsettling to say the least.

We worked at a bar run by a white owner, and were surrounded by a world of booze, drugs, corruption and modern-day slavery.

We watched someone die. We were shocked at the indifference of the locals towards death, the lack of hospital services and the attitude of the police, who were more interested in the contents of the dying man's pockets than in finding someone who could help him.

So yes, we worked in Uganda. It was an experience, an eye-opener, and something we would never want to do again.

We think it important to warn our readers of our experiences. Be prepared.

General Information

Capital: Kampala
Language Spoken: English and Swahili
Population: 40,046,754 (April 2016)
Religion: Roman Catholic 41.9%, Protestant 42% (Anglican 35.9%, Pentecostal 4.6%, Seventh Day Adventist 1.5%), Muslim 12.1%, other 3.1%, none 0.9%
Currency: Ugandan Shilling (UGX)
ATM: Barclays, Equity and KCB
Electricity: 240V, Type G
Climate: Rainy seasons are from March to June and October to December, but due to the high altitude, the climate is very pleasant.
Time Zone: UTC +3
Country Code: +256
Shops: Big supermarkets like Nakumatt and Shoprite, as well as small local stalls

Visa

Visas are required.

Cost: US$50/single entry, US$100/multiple entry
Validity: 90 days/single entry, 6–12 months/

multiple entry
Where to Get One: At the border

Travelling by Car

Carnet

You will need a carnet.

Car Insurance

COMESA

Road Tax

UGX 52,000 (payable on entry)

Road Condition

Ugandans drive on the left. Generally speaking, the roads are in good condition. There are only a few tarmac roads, but the gravel roads are in great condition and allow speeds up to 100 km/h (60 mph). In remote areas, the roads are deteriorating.

Police

You have three kinds of police in Uganda. The ones you have to watch out for wear bright white uniforms (don't ask us how they keep them white). They are the road police. Just remember to always stay nice and calm. We didn't have any problems with them, apart from the occasional check of our driving licenses.

Fuel

No problems getting fuel, either diesel or petrol.

Car Help

Toyota Uganda Limited

Address: Kampala First St, Kampala, Uganda

Phone: +256 (0)31 226 5563

Crossing the Border

Kenya–Uganda

We crossed at Busia. It took us an hour.

Formalities

Kenyan Side

- Get carnet stamped.
- Go to immigration department and fill out departure form.
- Fingerprints and picture.
- Get passport stamped.

Ugandan Side

- Get carnet stamped.
- Fill out entry form for Uganda.
- Fingerprints.
- Visa stamp: US$50.

Info

The lady who had to stamp our passport decided to make our border crossing difficult. She asked us what we were going to do in Uganda and how long we wanted to stay. We said we wanted to stay for three months (the maximum time on the visa), but she said that that wasn't possible and that she had never issued a three-month visa.

We found this to be a pretty stressful situation, as she was the one in charge and she was the one who would decide how long we got to stay. And you're not allowed to argue.

In cases such as these, remain polite and patient and smile, smile, smile! It also helps to say 'hello, how are you today' the moment you arrive. After 10 minutes of her refusing and our replies of, 'oh we didn't know that, friends of us stayed here for three months', and, 'oh we would love to stay three months, as everyone says that your country is amazing', 'there is so much to see here, we really hoped that we could stay for three months to see all the incredible sights you have in your country'… we finally got our three-month visas. Practice makes perfect!

Our Recommendations

There are a lot of hotels to choose from and a few campsites as well. Camping is often allowed on the hotel grounds if you ask, especially in rural areas.

Jinja

Jinja is a lovely place, very beautiful and quiet, especially if you have just come from busy Kampala.

Things to Do
Rafting on the Nile

I've rafted before, but I think rafting on the Nile was one of the best experiences I've had so far. You can choose which group you want to be in, rough or smooth. We went rough. It was AMAZING! You can arrange rafting at most backpackers' haunts in town.

Kampala

If you want to go for a short trip or out for a night, Kampala is full of 'boda bodas' (motorcycle-taxis). We took plenty of them, but be careful, as traffic in Kampala can be hectic. If you don't feel safe, shout to the driver to slow down. If he doesn't, tell him to stop, get off and pay him. If you take one at night, make sure your driver is sober. Many nightclubs in Kampala have their own bodas hanging out in the front and they are (on the whole) trustworthy.

Things to Do

There is some great nightlife in Kampala; every night is party night. We preferred Acacia Avenue in Kololo, where there are a lot of fantastic places.

Camping
Red Chilli Hideaway

> **Coordinates:** N02° 16.392' E31° 33.531'
> **Price:** US$8 per person per night
> **Address:** 13-23 Bukasa Hill View Road, Butabika, Kampala, Uganda
> **Phone 1:** +256 (0)77 250 9150
> **Phone 2:** +256 (0)31 220 2903
> **Email:** reservations@redchillihideaway.com
> **Website:** redchillihideaway.com

Since we were there, this campsite has relocated, so we can't really give a review of the new premises.

Bwindi National Park

Things to Do
Gorilla Trekking

The only reason we went to Bwindi was to see the gorillas. The road from Kampala to Bwindi has some stunning scenery. There are six places where you can go to see gorillas.

You will need to book your tickets beforehand at Kampala Wildlife Centre in Kampala. Tickets are cheaper in the rainy season. It's a pricy experience, but well worth it! Seeing gorillas up close is incredible!

Ticket prices 2016: US$600 pp and US$450 pp in the rainy season (April, May and November).

Ugandan Wildlife Authority

Address: Kira road plot 7, Kampala
Phone: +256 (0)41 435 5000
Opening Hours: Weekdays 8:00 a.m. to 4:30 p.m. and weekends from 10:00 a.m. to 12:30 p.m.
Website: www.ugandawildlife.org

Tanzania

Our Experience

If you come from the north, you will see the difference as soon as you drive into Tanzania. The roads are good and well maintained—there's tarmac all over!—and suddenly there are cyclists everywhere.

We liked Tanzania. We felt that the people were nicer and more honest and they didn't try to rip us off all the time. It's beautiful here—beautifully green.

However, we did have some communication troubles, as English isn't widely spoken here. You will find a lot of people here who don't speak any English at all.

General Info

Capital: Dodoma (not Dar es Salaam, but all major state-run offices are situated in Dar es Salaam)
Language Spoken: English and Swahili, but mostly Swahili.
Population: 27.4 million
Religion: Mainland: Christian 30%, Muslim 35%, indigenous beliefs 35%; Zanzibar: more than 99% Muslim

Currency: Tanzanian Shilling
ATM: NBC bank
Electricity: 230V, Type D and G
Climate: It is very humid along the coast from December to March. Rainy season is from March to May and in November. In central regions, the rainy season falls between January and April.
Time Zone: UTC +3
Country Code: +255
Shops: In Kenya and Uganda, you will find big supermarkets, but in Tanzania, they suddenly disappear. Once again, you will have to depend upon small street stalls and marketplaces.

Visa

Visas are required for almost all nationalities.

Cost: US$50 single entry
Validity: 90 days
Where to Get One: At the border

Travelling by Car

Car Insurance
COMESA

Carnet
You will need a carnet.

Road Conditions
Tanzanians drive on the left. Generally speaking, the roads are in good condition. Major routes in the north are made of tarmac, but there are a lot of gravel roads which are in bad condition, especially in the south.

Police

Lots of speed checks in this country, so watch your speed!

Fuel

No problems getting fuel; diesel and petrol are available.

Road Tax

US$25, paid at the border.

Car Help

CMC Automobiles

> **Address:** Maktaba Road, Dar es Salaam, Tanzania
> **Phone:** +255 (0)22 211 3017
> **Email:** cmc@cmcautomobiles.com
> **Note:** Official Landrover dealer

Toyota Tanzania Limited

> **Address:** Sokoine Dr, Dar es Salaam, Tanzania
> **Phone:** +255 (0)77 911 1555
> **Email:** sales@toyotatz.com

Other Info

Reflective strips are obligatory on the front and the rear of your vehicle, and you must have two emergency triangles. (See more about this in Chapter 2: Vehicle.)

Crossing the Border

Kenya–Tanzania

The easiest border we've had to cross so far (coming from the north). No-one came running trying to 'help' us, no hassled us and we felt very comfortable leaving our car alone.

Formalities
Kenyan Side
- First, you arrive at what we think was the old border, where you have to get your carnet stamped.
- Then you drive 6 km (4 miles) further to the real border.
- Here, they take a picture and scan your fingerprints.
- Then they stamp your visa.

Tanzania Side
- Fill in the entry paper.
- They take your picture.
- Scan your fingerprints.
- Pay visa stamp: US$50.
- Get carnet stamped.
- Pay US$25 road tax.

Our Recommendations

There are a lot of hotels and campsites along the coast. Camping is also often allowed within hotel grounds if you ask, especially in rural areas.

Tanza

Camping
Peponi Beach Resort

Coordinates: S05° 17.230' E39° 03.936'
Price: US$6.50 pp + US$1.50 pp tourism tax
Address: Located 30 km (18 miles) south of Tanga, and 14 km (8.5 miles) north of Pangani on the northern Tanzanian coast.
Phone 1: +255 (0)71 354 0139
Phone 2: +255 (0)76 593 0717
Email: info@peponiresort.com
Website: www.peponiresort.com
Facebook:
www.facebook.com/pages/Peponi-Beach-Camp-Lodge/275127832525501

Nice campsite between trees and next to a lake. They have a bar/restaurant on-site and they also offer some activities. Power is available for US$1/24 hrs and internet for US$2/day.

Bagamoyo

Camping

New Bagamoyo

Coordinates: S06° 25.831' E38° 54.177'
Price: US$9 pp
Address: Bagamoyo, Tanzania, located 756 km (470 miles) north of the city of Dar Es Salaam.
Phone: +255 (0)23 244 0083
Mobile: +255 (0)78 326 1655
Email: newbagamoyo@hotmail.com

Facebook:
www.facebook.com/NewBagamoyoBeachResort

This is a nice camping ground run by three Belgian guys. When we were there, they were still working on the pool and new toilet/shower facilities, as well as a cocktail bar on the beach. There are two toilets and a shower next to a little gym, but they were planning to build more. New Bagamoyo has a well-equipped bar/restaurant with beach view.

If you walk 300 metres along the beach, you will find a little market selling fresh fish—give it a go! Power is available at the bar and Wi-Fi at reception.

DO NOT GO:
Silver Sand Campsite
Price: US$6 pp

We stayed here, but don't recommend it. It's a large place, but very run-down and it isn't fenced off.

Sunrise Beach Resort
Coordinates: S6° 50.988' E39° 21.515'
Price for Camping: US$10 pp

We passed by to check it out, but the campsite was very close to the beach area where people were partying. Because of the noise, we didn't stay here.

Dar Es Salaam

Camping
Kipepeo Village

Coordinates: S6° 51.102' E39° 21.697'
Price: US$9.50 pp
Phone 1: +255 (0)71 375 7515
Phone 2: +255 (0)71 680 1383
Phone 3: +255 (0)75 427 6178
Website: www.kipepeovillage.com
Email: Info@KipepeoVillage.com

It's right on the beach, but there is a fence between beach

and campsite, which isn't that great. The staff quarters are also on the campsite and the occupants start making (a lot of) noise at 7 a.m. (and the cockerel starts to crow, too). Power available for US$5/24 hrs.

Internet is available for 4,500 TZS for 200 MB, valid for 24 hrs.

To get here (coming from Dar Es Salam), you will have to take a very short ferry ride, but due to queues, the journey can take up to one hour.

Price: 2,000 TZS/car + 200 TZS/passenger

Morogoro

Things to See

APOPO is a non-profit organisation which trains African giant-pouched rats to save lives by finding landmines or detecting tuberculosis. They have a training and research centre in Morogoro, which you can visit to see how they train these rats.

We went and were stunned at what they achieve here. It was very interesting to learn about the project and what the training involves. Rat training starts very early in the morning (before it gets too hot). You can visit the mine-detection rat training field from 7 a.m., or the TB detection rats from 10 a.m.

Visits are by appointment only and a donation of 120,000 TZS (or €60) is requested; this amount includes the adoption of one of the rats. It's a non-profit organisation, so your donation will be used within the programme and to save lives.

Website: www.apopo.org
Contact: herorats@apopo.org

Camping

There aren't really any camping sites in Morogoro, but if you want to see the rats in the morning, you will want to stay close by as that's early! There are several 'guesthouses' which are pretty cheap, so you can park your vehicle at the front and sleep inside. If you prefer to camp (like us) the only alternative we came across was a guesthouse opposite 'The Rock Garden'. It's not a camping ground at all; it's a guesthouse, but it has a garden. It wasn't the ideal place to set up camp, but it seemed to be the only option in town.

Iringa

Things to See

Stone Age Site

Next to the Isimila African Garden campsite is the 'Stone Age Site', which is beautiful, but they recently changed their entrance fee from 5,000 to 20,000 TZS. Although it is beautiful, we personally don't think it's worth that higher price.

Camping

Isimila African Garden

Coordinates: S07° 53.581' E035° 36.236'

Price: US$6 per adult, US$3 per child (6–16 years), free for children up to five years of age.
Phone 1: +255 (0)77 951 8772
Phone 2: +255 (0)77 424 2692
Email: info@isimila-african-garden.com
Website: isimila-african-garden.com
Facebook:
https://www.facebook.com/Isimila-African-Garden-317044321662274

Another nice place that's currently being renovated. They have a lovely sitting area/bar. We were allowed to use a toilet and a shower in one of the rooms. When we were there, the showers were still cold, but they were working on a solar system to heat the water. Power is available at the bar.

Mbeya

Camping
Karibuni Centre

Coordinates: S08° 54.559' E33° 26.637'
Price: 5,000 TZS pp
Phone: +255 (0)25 250 3035
Email: mec@maf.or.tz
Website:
www.twiga.ch/TZ/karibunicenter.htm

This is the only nice place we could find close to the Malawi border that allowed camping. This place is inexpensive and has nice, basic, cheap food in the bar. You're not allowed to drive on the grass and you have to camp in the car park. Power is available at the restaurant.

Malawi

Our Experience

Malawi is amazing—so green! The people are super friendly and, compared to other countries in which we travelled, the majority of them are honest—they don't try to get their hands on your money the moment they see you are a foreigner. It's striking that Malawi is a poor country, but alcohol and cigarettes are extremely cheap and you will often come across drunks. Children sadly come into contact with alcohol at an early age. However, even this did not take away the fact that, as overlanders, we thoroughly enjoyed Malawi—it is so beautiful and many of its national parks are free!

General Information

Capital: Lilongwe
Language Spoken: English and Chichewa
Population: 17,6 million
Religion: Christian 79.9%, Muslim 12.8%, other 3%, none 4.3%
Currency: Malawian kwacha (MWK)
ATM: Standard Bank and NBS Bank
Note: If you cross the border from Tanzania

(Songwe), it's 50 km (30 miles) to the first ATM in Karonga (National Bank of Malawi (S09° 56.102' E033° 56.545'). We advise you to change some money before entering Malawi if you're not planning on driving straight to Karonga.

Electricity: 230V, Type G

Climate: Very pleasant. Rainy season is from November to March.

Time Zone: UTC +2

Country Code: +265

Shops: Shoprite, Chipiku Plus, Chipiku Stores, Metro Cash n Carry, Peoples.

Health: Yellow fever vaccination is required if you are coming from at risk countries such as Uganda, Sudan, Kenya and Ethiopia. Find a full list on www. who.int.

Visa

As of October 1, 2015, Malawi has introduced new visa requirements to include nationals from countries where Malawians are required to pay for visas. Most nationals of European countries (excluding Ireland) and the US will need a visa.

Cost: US$75 for single entry, US$150 for multiple entry.

Duration: Three months for single entry, six months for multiple entry.

Where to Get One: At the border.

Travelling by Car

Carnet

You will need a carnet.

Car Insurance
COMESA

As of March 2016, the following are required when entering Malawi with a vehicle:

- Third-party insurance—obtained at the border at a cost of 21,000 MWK.
- Temporary importation permit—obtained at the border at a cost of 10,000 MWK.

(Source: www.malawitourism.com)

Road Conditions
Drive on the left. Generally speaking, the roads are in a reasonable condition. Surprisingly, there is very little traffic, especially in the north. This may be due to frequent fuel shortages.

Police
Didn't come across any problems.

Fuel
Fuel is expensive here and prices include various taxes, so top up everything you have with you before entering Malawi. When we were here in 2013, fuel was US$0.70 per litre more expensive in Malawi than it was in Tanzania.

Car Help
Toyota Blantyre
>**Coordinates:** S15° 48.173' E35° 02.938'
>**Address:** Blantyre, Malawi
>**Phone 1:** +265 (0)1 841 933
>**Phone 2:** +265 (0)1 841 726

Phone 3: +265 (0)1 841 726
Email: customercare@toyotamalawi.com

Toyota Lilongwe
Address: Kenyatta, Lilongwe, Malawi
Phone 1: +265 (0)1 755 666
Phone 2: +265 (0)1 755 661
Phone 3: +265 (0)1 755 669
Email: customercare@toyotamalawi.com

Toyota Malawi Limited
Coordinates: S11° 27.815' E33° 59.823'
Address: Katoto, Along M1 Road, Mzuzu, Malawi
Phone 1: +265 (0)1 841 933
Phone 2: +265 (0)1 841 726
Email: customercare@toyotamalawi.com

Crossing the Border
Tanzania–Malawi
Border Used
Songwe

Formalities
Tanzanian Side
- Fill in exit form and carnet.

Malawian Side
- Fill in entry form and carnet.
- Take fingerprints, no pictures.
- Very fast.

Note
In 2013, this was a very simple and fast procedure, as visas were not required. Now that visas are obligatory and car

import fees must be processed and paid, expect the procedure to be longer.

Our Recommendations

There are hotels and campsites along the banks of Lake Malawi.

Camping is also often permitted on hotels' grounds if you ask nicely, especially in more rural areas.

In the more remote areas, accommodations are few and far between.

Karonga

Things to See
Karonga Museum

Coordinates: S09° 56.489' E33° 55.392'
Facebook: www.facebook.com/CMCK.Malawi
Email: karongamuseum@gmail.com
Phone 1: +265 (0)88 851 5574
Phone 2: +265 (0)99 323 4000
Phone 3: +265 (0)88 886 1014
Phone 4: +265 (0)99 538 6932
Opening Hours: Mon–Sat: 9:00–17:00, Sun: 13:00–17:00

This is a small but interesting museum with a 130-million-year-old Malawisaurus (dinosaur) fossil as its star exhibit.

Camping
Karonga-Mufawa Lakeside Lodge (Taj Hotel)

Coordinates: S09° 56.234' E33° 56.678'
Price: 1,500 MWK pp

This is a big local hotel with a large garden. We stayed in the garden and were allowed to use one of the rooms' bathroom. The toilet was OK, but I wouldn't shower there.

The owner was extremely friendly and very happy to have us stay. You can walk or take a bike-taxi to the local market.

Chtimba

Camping

Chitimba Lodge and Camp

Coordinates: S10° 35.077' E34° 10.541'
Price: US$6 pp
Website: www.chitimba.com
Email: camp@chitimba.com
Phone: +265 (0)88 838 7116

This is a very popular place with tourists and it can get very busy. A lot of large overland trucks stop here, which we weren't very enthusiastic about, as they meant too many people and way too much noise. There is a nice bar with TVs. The major drawback was that they only had a cold shower. But it is right on Lake Malawi. The owners are from the Netherlands.

Hakuna Matata

Coordinates: S10° 35.148' E34° 10.510'
Price: US$6 pp
Facebook:
www.facebook.com/hakunamatata.chitimba
Email:
hakunamatata.chitimba@gmail.com

Phone 1: +265 (0)88 126 2338
Phone 2: +265 (0)88 126 2337
Note: Phone calls don't always go through due to the weak signal.

This place is right next to Chitimba Lodge and Camp and we loved it! Primarily, because it's smaller and without all the overland trucks. And … they had a HOT shower!

The owner's name is Willy, an old man who repeats himself a lot, but who is extremely friendly! His right hand is Maggi, who keeps an eye on administration and the kitchen.

They don't have a fancy bar like next door, but Maggi can cook you some tasty local dishes. They also have an old computer with very slow internet.

This place is right on the banks of Lake Malawi.

Willy was also kind enough to help us out with fuel. He called a friend who brought us fuel when we were getting low.

Livingstonia

Things to See and Do
Chombe Plateau
The spectacular Chombe Plateau offers stunning 360-degree views of Lake Malawi, Nyika National Park and the surrounding mountain ranges.

Lukwe Permaculture Gardens
Less than a mile (1.3 km) from the Mushroom Farm on the main Livingstonia road, you will find the Lukwe

Permaculture Gardens. The ponds and eco-gardens here provide a shining example of the self-sufficient possibilities Malawi is capable of.

Coffee Farm Tours

Ever thought about where your coffee comes from? Interested in natural farming techniques in Malawi? Spend the day with local guide McDonald, exploring local smallholder coffee plantations and a permaculture farm based in Vungu-Vungu, 5 km (3 miles) from the Mushroom Farm.

Manchewe Waterfalls and Caves

Situated just over a mile (2 km) from the Mushroom Farm, on the main Livingstonia road, is Malawi's tallest waterfall, Manchewe Falls. Surrounded by rainforest, they drop 100 meters into the gorge.

Historic Livingstonia

Perched above Lake Malawi and the Rift Valley escarpment lies the historic town of Livingstonia. Originally founded by Scottish missionaries in the late 19th century, Livingstonia offers breathtaking views and a historic look into past settlements.

Eat Local Cuisine at Manchewe Village

Enjoy a relaxing and affordable lunch while supporting local restaurants in Manchewe village. Please allow some time for food preparation—it's well worth the wait!

(Source: www.themushroomfarmmalawi.com)

Camping
Lukwe EcoCamp & Organic Gardens

Coordinates: S10° 33.341' E34° 07.616'
Price: US$6 (4,500 MWK)
Website: www.lukwe.com
Email: Lukwe@live.com
Phone: +265 (0)99 943 4985

The road up to the campsite is steep and a bit scary, but this place is well worth the trip! Lukwe EcoCamp & Organic Gardens is run by a friendly Belgian guy. There are a few campsites on the level ground, with shelter. Check out the bar—it's an awesome spot! It has been built right on the edge of the mountain, where you can sit on a swing and dangle over the edge. A lovely place for a quiet drink.

There are also a few lodges, which the owner (Auke) runs more as a hobby than to make a big profit. He likes to keep it small, which results in a minimum of travellers and a peaceful environment. He's happy for you to bring your own drinks to the bar; as he says, if you drink his beer, he has to go all the way down the mountain to get new ones.

The Mushroom Farm

Coordinates: S10° 35.197' E34° 08.069'
Price: US$5 pp
Website: www.themushroomfarmmalawi.com
Facebook:
www.facebook.com/themushroomfarmmalawi
Email:
themushroomfarmmalawi@gmail.com
Phone: +265 (0)99 965 2485

This campsite is just down the road from Lukwe EcoCamp. We weren't here ourselves, but heard a lot of good things about it.

Mzuzu

Things to See
Vwaza Wildlife Reserve
Coordinates: S11° 08.106' E33° 39.360'
Price: US$5 pp + 1% tourism tax
Camping: 1,750 MWK pp

This is supposed to be a national park where you can see a lot of elephants. Yes, we saw elephants ... dead ones. We saw the remains of what the poachers left behind, the sight of which has been burned into our memories forever ...

But apart from that, this is a very cheap national park. We slept alongside the lake, where a herd of hippos were having a snooze. There were also a lot of buffalos. It's quite a small park.

Camping
Mozoozoo

Coordinates: S11° 27.425' E34° 01.677'
Price: 1,000 MWK pp
Address: Kaning'Ina street, Mzuzu

Facebook: www.facebook.com/Mzoozoozoo
Phone: +265 (0)88 886 4493

This place is close to the centre of town and you can park your car at the back of the compound. It is run by an old man, who smokes and swears from the comfort of his wheelchair. They have a bar and also serve food.

We stayed here because we had to wait for car parts, otherwise we wouldn't have bothered as it's not the nicest place for overlanders.

Silver Grey Lodge

Coordinates: S11° 29.43' E38° 58.088'
Price: 1,000 MWK pp

This one is a bit further out. You can park your car outside, in the forest. The surrounding scenery is nicer than Mozoozoo, but there aren't any fences around the terrain, so curious local kids will just walk in to have a stare.

Nkhata Bay

Things to Do
Diving with Aqua Africa

Coordinates: S11° 36.497' E34° 18.031'
Price: US$350 pp
Website: www.aquaafrica.co.uk
Phone: +265 (0)99 992 1418

We decided to learn how to dive in Africa rather than in Europe.

The water in Malawi is always warm compared to Belgium and you get to see a lot of fish right from the start! We researched a few companies and ended up using Aqua Africa, with which we were very happy!

We learned to dive in a small group of four; very personal and a lot of fun. At lunchtime, we would go into the village and try out the local restaurants.

The diving instructors also picked us up every morning and dropped us off in the evening. Even if you don't dive, you should still stop at Aqua Africa to try some of their delicious chocolate cake!

Camping
Njaya Lodge Campsite

Coordinates: S11° 37.241' E34° 18.301'
Price: US$5 pp + 1% tourism tax
Website: <u>www.njayalodge.com</u>
Email: <u>info@njayalodge.com</u>
Phone: +265 (0)88 474 3647

This is the only campsite in town with enough space for you to camp in your rooftop tent. Nice grassy area, but unfortunately a lot of ants! They have a lovely bar/restaurant and the beach is just onwards from the bar.

Nkhotakota

Camping

Nkhota Kota Pottery Lodge

Coordinates: S13° 03.018' E34° 19.576'
Price: 1,600 MWK pp
Website: www.nkhotakota-pottery-lodge.com
Phone: +265 (0)88 458 1098
Mobile: +265 (0)99 718 9064

The campsite is fenced off from the beach, but it's a nice place.

The only drawback is the constant presence of local kids hanging on the fence to stare and shout at you.

DO NOT GO

Butterfly and Mayota Village.

They don't have the space for overlanders.

Cape Maclear

Things to See

If you drive from Lilongwe to Monkey Bay, you will see locals selling wooden cars along the road. It's worth stopping to have a look around to find a miniature version of your own vehicle! Very, very pretty and a great souvenir.

Camping
Fat Monkey

Coordinates: S14° 01.462' E34° 50.503'
Price: US$6 pp (US$3 for a small tent)
Website: fatmonkeysmw.com
Email: fatmonkeys@esafrican.com
Phone: +265 (0)88 045 3666

Lovely setting right on the beach, but a VERY tiny campsite. As a lot of Namibians and South Africans travel around southern Africa right up to Malawi, so you will find a lot of them here. (Their fancy cars will take up a lot more space than yours!)

This is also a popular spot with backpackers. It wasn't our favourite campsite, but it was handy to have Internet (Skyband hotspot 1,200 MWK for 200 MB) for once.

Lilongwe

Things to Do
Lilongwe Wildlife Centre
www.lilongwewildlife.org

This is Malawi's only wildlife sanctuary dedicated to protecting Malawi's wildlife and habitats.

The centre takes care of animals rescued by the Government, primarily from illegal wildlife trades.

Lilongwe Wildlife Centre is situated in the heart of the capital city. Find them on Kenyatta Drive between Old Town and the City Centre.

DON'T MISS
Malawi is full of bikes and bike-taxis, so try one out! It's very cheap and one hell of an experience.

Camping
Golf Club

Coordinates: S13° 59.499' E33° 46.11'
Price: US$5 pp
Email: info@lilongwegolfclub.com
Phone: +265 (0)1 753 598

On the golf course, they have made a little campsite with fire pits. They also have tennis and squash courts and a swimming pool that you can use for a fee. There's a bar where you can use electricity and internet.

They also have a small workshop where they helped us out by carrying out a small welding job on our car.

Mabuya Camp

Price: US$7 pp
Website: www.mabuyacamp.com

Email: info@mabuyacamp.com
Phone: +265 (0)88 045 3666

This is a backpacker's place where you can camp in the car park. They have two spots on the gravel. The car park is in front of the building, so everyone was always passing by. Because of this lack of privacy, we decided not to stay here.

Zambia

Our Experience

Zambia is beautiful, but more expensive than most African countries. National parks are expensive here, but you can see some pretty nice wildlife when camping just outside the parks and of course, don't miss the incredible waterfalls!

General Information

Capital: Lusaka
Language Spoken: Nyanja/Bemba
Population: 16.6 million
Religion: Christian 50%–75%, Muslim and Hindu 24%–49%, indigenous beliefs 1%
Currency: Zambian Kwatcha (ZKW)
ATM: Barclays, Finance Bank, Zanaco
Electricity: 230V, Type C, D, and G
Climate: Tropical, modified by altitude. Rainy season is from October to April.
Time Zone: UCT +2
Country Code: +260
Shops: Spar, Shoprite and Pick 'n Pay as well as local stalls and markets

Visa

Cost: US$50 for single entry, US$80 for multiple entry.
Duration Single Entry: 30 days
Duration Multiple Entry: 90 days
Where to Get One: At the border

Travelling by Car

Carnet

Get the stamp in the same building where you get your visa and pay the carbon tax. You will need a receipt for the carbon tax before you can get your carnet stamped.

Car Insurance

Third-party insurance, costing 150 ZKW or US$30 for one month. It's cheaper to pay in ZKW.

Carbon Tax

- You will have to pay this in the building where you got your visa.
- Fill in the book.
- Pay 150 ZKW (the price depends on the vehicle type). You have to pay this in ZKW.
- You will be given a receipt.

Road Tax

You pay this in a separate building. It will be necessary to tell them which border you are going to use as an exit. As we didn't know and after a bit of small talk, the person handling this wrote down three different borders.

Fee: US$20 which has to be paid in US$.

Road Conditions

Mainly tarmac roads.

Police

There are a LOT of speed controls, so watch your speed!

Fuel

Widely available.

Car Help

Toyota Zambia, Nangwenya Road

Address: Thabo Mbeki Rd, Lusaka, Zambia
Phone: +260 (0)21 137 8051

Lusaka Toyota

Address: Northend Cairo Road, Lusaka
Phone: +260 (0)21 137 8051
Email: contactus@toyotazambia.co.zm

Alliance Motors Zambia (JLR)

Address: Plot 9219 Ben Bella Road, Lusaka
Phone 1: +260 (0)21 184 7991
Phone 2: +260 (0)21 184 6917
Email: sales@alliancemotors.co.zm
Note: Official Landrover dealer

Other Info

Reflective strips on the front and the rear of the vehicle are obligatory, as well as two emergency triangles.

(See more about this in Chapter 2: Your Vehicle.)

Crossing the Border
Malawi–Zambia
Border Used
Mgabi

Formalities
Malawi Side
- Exit stamp in visa (no exit form).
- Exit stamp carnet.

Note: Very fast, only took 10 min.

Zambia Side
- Fill in entry in book.
- Stamp visa.
- Stamp carnet.
- Pay road tax and carbon tax.

Our Recommendations

Chipata

Camping
Dean's Hill View

Coordinates: S13° 38.090' E32° 37.594'
Price: 35 ZKW pp
Address: Chipata Welcome Arch, 500 metres (546

yards) off the main Lusaka Highway, Chipata, Zambia
Phone: +260 (0)97 172 0686
Email: contact@deanshillviewlodge.com
Website: deanshillviewlodge.com

This camping is indeed up a hill. It's a nice, big, grassy area, but it's a bit hard to find a flat surface. There is a little kitchen that you can use, where you can find power points.

Mfuwe

Camping
Track and Trail River Camp

Coordinates: S13° 06.056' E31° 47.441'
Price: US$12.50 pp
Email: info@trackandtrailrivercamp.com
Phone: +260 (0)21 624 6020
Mobile 1: +260 (0)97 760 0556
Mobile 2: +260 (0)97 424 4850
Website: www.trackandtrailrivercamp.com
Facebook:
www.facebook.com/TrackandTrailrivercamp

The price was more than we usually paid, but SO worth it! The Track and Trail River Camp is just outside the national park, which means you can see the wildlife for free. You will even spot a lot of animals on the drive up to the campsite.

They have a nice pool overlooking a river where crocodiles

like to sunbathe. They also have a really nice bar and seating overlooking the river.

As soon as it gets dark, a guard appears to escort you from your tent to the bar and back again, as elephants tend to visit the campsite (which they did when we were there).

We had to walk around them going to and from the bar. Either we passed them, or they passed us as we sat at the bar. Back in our tent, we could hear them eating the tree branches just a few metres away.

It was an incredible experience!

Nyimba

Camping
Chimwewe Lodge

Coordinates: S14° 17.655' E31° 20.338'
Price: US$10 pp
Address: Boma Road, 400 km (248 miles) east of Lusaka, along the Petauke, turn off from Great East Road, Petauke, Zambia
Phone: +260 (0)21 637 1545
Mobile 1: +260 (0)96 880 7900
Mobile 2: +260 (0)97 776 2041
Email: info@chimwemwelodge.com
Website: www.chimwemwelodge.com

Lusaka

Camping

Pioneer Camp

Coordinates: S15° 23.778' E28° 27.036'
Price: US$10 pp
Phone: +260 (0)96 643 2700
Email: mail@pioneercampzambia.com
Website: www.pioneercampzambia.com
Facebook: www.facebook.com/PioneerLusaka

Nice place with a big grassy area under the trees for camping. They also have a lovely restaurant and a bar that offers free tea and coffee all day. There is also a little swimming pool and a TV area.

Power points are available in the TV area or the restaurant.

You will be able to do your washing in a REAL washing machine here!

Full Load: 50 ZKW
Half Load: 30 ZKW

Eureka Camp

Coordinates: S15° 30.164' E28° 15.904'

Price: 40 ZKW pp
Address: 10 km (5 miles) south of Lusaka City centre, on the Kafue Road, Lusaka, Zambia
Phone: +260 (0)21 127 8110
Mobile 1: +260 (0)96 682 2448
Mobile 2: +260 (0)97 780 3051
Email: eurekacamp.zm@gmail.com
Website: www.eurekacamp.com

Nice, big camping ground with a lot of little shelters that you can use in case of rain.

You will also see zebras and giraffes within the campsite. This was a nice extra, but felt a bit strange, as the campsite is close to the city and surrounded by busy roads.

Lake Kariba

Camping
Eagles Rest Resort

Coordinates: S16° 32.119' E28° 43.767'
Price: 60 ZKW pp
Address: Plot 218, N/A Siavonga, Lake Kariba
Phone: +260 (0)97 886 9126
Email: eagles@siavonga-zambia.com
Website: www.eaglesrestresort.com
Facebook: www.facebook.com/eagles.rest.siavonga

When we were here, we had the entire place to ourselves. Lovely!

It has a nice swimming pool and is just a short walk to the beach.

They have Internet available for 9 ZKW/hour.

It's only a short drive to Kariba Dam, which is an impressive sight!

Copperbelt

Things to See
Chimfunshi

After getting out of our vehicle, we found ourselves surrounded by a bunch of ducks waddling around, two sheep came to have a sniff at our clothes, three dogs came for some attention, and a monkey jumped on our car and started biting into our rooftop tent ... Then a gigantic dog stormed towards us, which scared the monkey, which jumped onto a sheep's back and then onto Dries' head!

A man with a chimpanzee on his back was watching our predicament. Then he suddenly shouted, 'welcome to the orphanage!'

This might tell you that Chimfunshi is a little bit different to other wildlife sanctuaries.

Chimfunshi is a chimpanzee orphanage with large enclosures where you can watch them. We would definitely recommend a visit.

Luckily, you can camp here for 100 ZKW pp. We drove up here from Lusaka and didn't see any campsites on the way.

Price: 50 ZKW pp

Address: Solwesi Road, Copperbelt, Zambia
Phone: +260 (0)96 856 8830
Email: enquiries@chimfunshiwildlife.org
Website: www.chimfunshi.de

Information

If you're using Tracks4Africa, it's best to take the road that starts at: S12° 26.583' E27°25.246'. There are a lot of potholes, so don't arrive after dark.

Kitwe

Things to See

Lilayi Elephant Nursery

Coordinates: S15° 31.800' E28° 18.610'
Cost: Donation

Camping
Zemics Ark

Coordinates: S12° 53.081' E28° 17.645'
Price: 50 ZKW pp
Address: Jambo Drive, Riverside, Kitwe, Zambia
Phone 1: +260 (0)21 222 2252
Phone 2: +260 (0)21 222 9584
Email: chrisbanda@zamtel.zm

Great North Road

Camping
Moorings Camp

Coordinates: S16° 11.671' E27° 32.590'
Price: 50 ZKW pp
Address: Monze, Zambia
Phone: +260 (0)21 325 5049
Mobile: +260 (0)97 752 1352
Email: tsavory@zamnet.zm
Website: mooringscampsite.com

Nice little campsite with small huts in which you can cook, sit and play games. It also has a little shop on-site with basic products.

Livingstone

Things to See
Victoria Falls
One of the most famous waterfalls in the world. Simply too amazing to miss.

Camping
Maramba River Lodge

Coordinates: S17° 53.349' E25° 51.329'
Price: US$10 pp
Address: Mosi au Tunya Rd, PO Box 60957, Livingstone, Zambia

Phone: +260 (0)21 332 4189
Mobile: +260 (0)97 658 7511
Email: reservations@marambariverlodge.com
Website: maramba-zambia.com
Facebook:
www.facebook.com/pages/Maramba-River
Lodge/222552617794324

A bit more expensive, but a very pleasant and clean campsite. They have a lovely pool and a bar that overlooks the river where hippos spend time, especially at night. There's a good chance that you will see elephants up close. From this campsite, you can take a taxi to the falls; it's not very expensive and this way, your vehicle remains safe. Wi-Fi available in the bar.

We also passed by Kubu Cabins and Camp Nkwazi, which are in a really nice setting, but quoted US$25 pp for camping, so we didn't stay.

Namibia

Our Experience

Namibia is beautiful and totally set up for tourists. A lot of
tourists come here with rented 'overland' cars. There are two
large, sealed roads that take you across the entire country. As
there are many tourist accommodations, they are also of a
higher standard than in other countries; nice little campsites
often with your own water supply and braai. Namibia is
a former German colony, as you will quickly discover. We

heard that there are even campsites in Namibia where only German-speaking people are allowed. Quite sad, really. Luckily, we didn't run into any of them!

General Information

Capital: Windhoek
Language Spoken: English, Oshiwambo
Population: 2,505,588 (April 2016)
Religion: Christian 80%–90% (Lutheran 50% at least), indigenous beliefs 10%–20%
Currency: Namibian dollar (N$) and South African rand both accepted, as well as US dollar.
ATM: Standard Bank and Barclays
Electricity: 220, Type D and M
Climate: Desert; hot, dry; rainfall is sparse and erratic.
Time Zone: UTC +1
Country Code: +264
Shops: Shoprite and Spar

Visa

Cost: Free
Duration: 90 days
Where to Get One: At the border

Travelling by Car
Carnet

Namibia, Botswana, South Africa, Lesotho and Swaziland form part of a common customs area called the Southern African Customs Union, or SACU.

As long as travellers remain in the SACU countries, they

only need to have their carnets stamped the first time they enter a SACU country, and then again once they leave the common customs area. No stamp is required when travelling from one SACU country to another.

Car Insurance

None, but you need to purchase road tax when entering; third-party insurance is included in the price of fuel.

Road Conditions

There are two main roads crossing through Namibia, very good tarmac ones where you can drive up to 100 km/h (60 mph). Aside from these two main roads, all the rest are sandy tracks. Roads are quite empty; not a lot of animals, bicycles or people running around. Along the roadside, you will find picnic spots where you can stop for a meal. Namibia is a very popular tourist spot, so you will see a lot of rented 4WD's (*always* white) pass you by. As these groups are proper tourists and in a hurry to see everything, they rarely have time to stop for a chat, or to help you out if you're having trouble with your car.

Police

We weren't stopped once by the police in Namibia except at at the border crossing.

Fuel

No problems getting fuel; diesel and petrol are available, but petrol stations might be far from each other, so best top up when you get the chance.

If you're crossing from Zambia, the first petrol station is in Katima. The next one is in Divundu, 300 km (185 miles) away. And the next one in Rundu is 500 km (310 miles) after that.

Vet Fence

In Namibia, 'vet fences' control the spread of animal diseases. In the north of Namibia, animal diseases are more common and you are not permitted to transport raw meat or animal products (such as unpasteurised milk) from north to south over the 'vet border'. If you travel from south to north, there is no problem. You are also not permitted to transport meat from west to east, but the opposite direction is not a problem.

At these fences, they will check your car for uncooked meat and animal products. If you would like to take meat over this border, it must be cooked. No raw meat, even if frozen or vacuum packed, may be taken over the border.

In Namibia, you are not allowed to transport raw meat from:

- Katima Mulilo to Rundu.
- Rundu to Grootfontein (vet fence S18° 47.640' E18° 55.705').
- Palmwag South into Damaraland. (S19° 14.529' E14° 25.081').
- From the vet fence, west between Tsumkwe and the main Rundu/Grootfontein road. (S18° 45.254' E18° 57.909').
- Etosha, if you're travelling north to south (vet fence S19° 14.533' E14° 25.080').

On Tracks4Africa's GPS maps, these fences are referred to as 'vet fences' and are indicated with red lines.

(Source: blog.tracks4africa.co.za/veterinary-fences-in-namibia-and-botswana)

Crossing the Border
Zambia–Namibia

Formalities

Zambian Side
- Stamp exit visa.
- Fill in the book.
- Carnet stamp.

Namibian Side
- Fill entry form.
- Stamp visa.
- Carnet stamp.
- Fill in form for CBC (Cross Border Charge).
- Pay N$220 for CBC.

Note

You won't be hassled. People are quite unfriendly on the Namibian side.

Our Recommendations

Namibia is a very popular destination for people from overseas, so keep in mind that when the school summer holidays are going on around July and August, there will be a lot more (European) tourists around. The school holidays in Namibia and South Africa (December and January) are a popular time for the locals to go travelling, so accommodation might fill up quickly.

Katima

Camping
Mukusi Cabins

Coordinates: S17° 30.136' E24° 16.206'
Price: N$70 pp
Address: B8, Katima Mulilo, Namibia
Phone: +264 (0)66 253 255
Mobile: +264 (0)81 127 4648
Email: mukusi@afol.com.na
Website: www.mukusi.com

Nice campsite behind the cabins, with a camp kitchen that has a working fridge! Nice bar for a drink. Wi-Fi and power available behind the bar.

Protea Hotel-Zambezi River Lodge

Coordinates: S17° 29.187' E24° 17.113'
Price: N$140 pp
Address: Ngoma Road, Caprivi Region Katima Mulilo 9000, Namibia
Phone: +264 (0)66 251 500
Website: www.marriott.com/hotels/travel/mpapr-

protea-hotel-zambezi-river-lodge

Next to the river. Each camp spot has its own braai and dishwashing area. There is free Wi-Fi (and power) in the bar, as well as a swimming pool.

Grootfontein

Things to See
Hoba Meteorite

Coordinates: S19° 35.585' E17° 56.059'
Price: N$25 pp

You can find this meteorite near Grootfontein. It's the largest known meteorite on Earth and weighs 60 tonnes!

Camping
Roy's Rest Camp

Coordinates: S19° 14.003' E18° 30.029'
Price: N$95 pp
Phone: +264 (0)67 240 302
Email: royscamp@iway.na
Website: www.roysrestcamp.com
Facebook: www.facebook.com/pages/Roys-Rest-Camp-Namibia/326550430735

Nice campsite; each site has its own table, electricity point, light and even a tap! There is also a bush kitchen if you feel like using it. Very nice and cosy bar and you can use internet for free here.

Etosha

Things to See
Etosha National Park

This is a very nice national park with a lot of wildlife. Expect to bump into zebras on ALL the roads.

>**Price:** N$80 pp per day, and N$10 per car per day
>**Website:** etoshanationalpark.co.za

You will come across a vet fence if you're travelling from north to south (vet fence S19° 14.533' E14° 25.08').

Camping
Halali, Namutoni, Okaukuejo

>**Coordinates:** S19° 03.545' E16° 47.124'
>**Price:** N$220 for up to eight people
>**Email:** enquiry@etoshanationalpark.org
>**Website:**
>www.etoshanationalpark.org/accommodation/
>halali-camp

This campsite is nothing special, just a big area with some braais and a few trees, but it can still get crowded. The main reason people come to this campsite is because of the waterhole that is lit up at night. At night, when it's dark and cool, animals will come to the waterhole for a drink; you might need to be patient, but your patience will definitely be rewarded! Power points in the restaurant.

Kamanjab

Kamanjab is the last major stop when travelling to Damaraland or Kaokoland.

On the way down to Kamanjab, you will pass a vet fence: S19° 14.529' E14° 25.081'.

Camping
Oppi Koppi Rest Camp

Coordinates: S19° 37.247' E14° 50.866'
Price: Free for overlanders!
Address: Kunene Region northwest Namibia. Oppi Koppi Rest Camp is situated 300 metres (328 yards) from the centre in Kamanjab at the junction of C40 and C35, Outjo-Palmwag, Ruancana-Khorixas.
Phone: +264 (0)67 330 040
Mobile: +264 (0)81 453 0958
Email: info@oppi-koppi-kamanjab.com
Website: www.oppi-koppi-kamanjab.com

Another positive side to being an overlander—camping here is free! But be on your guard; because it's free, you might think, 'let's have a drink or a meal as we saved on camping'. Then you have another drink to congratulate yourself for your finding this place. And then another. We ended up spending more than we usually would for a camping pitch, but it was worth it.

The owner is a very friendly Belgian guy with lots of stories to tell and the regulars will also keep you amused at the bar. They also have a swimming pool and free Wi-Fi in the restaurant.

Otjititongwe Cheetah Lodge

Coordinates: S19° 35.498' E15° 04.003'
Price: N$300 pp for camping, with the cheetah tour included.
Address: Kamanjab, Namibia, 24 km (14 miles) east of Kamanjab and only 8 km (5 miles) from the junction C40 north on road P2683
+264 (0)67 330 201
Email: cheetahs@iway.na

The strange thing here is that it's cheaper to camp here and go on the cheetah tour, than to go on the cheetah tour without camping (don't ask us why). The campsite is nothing special, but the cheetah tour is very impressive. You will first be allowed to pet their 'tame' cheetahs (cheetahs that were rescued when they were very young and are now unable to return to the wild) before being taken on a tour of the property to show you their breeding program.

We are absolutely anti-tourist-attractions where wild animals are used as a means of tourist entertainment and we would normally never join a 'pet the wild cat' tour. But we hope you will forgive us, as we hadn't expected to be so close to these beautiful animals.

However, this organisation is doing a very good job in maintaining cheetah populations in Namibia. We did have mixed feelings after our visit, but thought we would make an exception here.

Epupa Falls

Camping

Epupa Falls-Omarunga Lodge

Coordinates: S17° 00.153' E13° 14.770'
Price: N$120 pp/day
Phone: +264 (0)81 620 6887

Email: bookings@damaraland-namibia.com
Website: www.omarungalodge.com
Facebook:
www.facebook.com/omarunga.lodge?fref=ts

Beautiful setting if you can get a spot facing the river (you can email or call them ahead of time to make a reservation). The only danger is falling branches from the palm trees above you.

Things to See

Epupa Falls
They are right next to the campsite, so you won't have to go far.

Himba Village

The campsite offers a tour to the local Himba village; it's rather expensive, but we really wanted to see it ... and we were very disappointed.

The village is totally geared towards tourists and the guide always tells the girls what to do so you can take pictures.

'Put the baby on your breast. Take picture, take picture. Rub your skin. Take picture, take picture.' We felt really, really uncomfortable.

We weren't visiting a village, we were visiting a zoo.

They've also set up a little market selling products they've made themselves, but they ask high prices and aren't open to haggling. You're better off buying the same goods in town from a local shop.

In exchange for us being allowed to visit their village, the campsite gives them food. This isn't even worth a fifth of the price we paid for the tour.

We felt bad afterwards and wished we'd never gone.

Sossusvlei

Things to See
Sossusvlei

Really stunning and worth the visit! This is something you just can't miss: the red sand dunes, the salt and clay pans ...

We climbed Dune 45 to watch the sunrise. The gate opens at 5:30 a.m. and the sun rises at about 6:15 a.m., so you have about 40 minutes to climb the dune. You need those 40 minutes! It's a difficult trek, as the sand is soft and there's a lot of wind. But it is so worth it!

Camping
Solitaire Camp

Coordinates: S23° 53.671' E16° 00.326'
Price: N$120 pp
Phone 1: +264 (0)61 305 173
Phone 2: +264 (0)61 305 176
Email: reservations@solitaireguestfarm.com
Website: www.solitaireguestfarm.com

This campsite is just outside the park, so if you want to see the sun rise over the dunes, this is the best place. When we were there, it was very windy and we hardly slept in our rooftop tent because of the wind. They have a restaurant with reasonably-priced food, which comes in handy when it's too windy to cook.

Windhoek

Camping
Chameleon BP

Price: N$100 pp
Address: 5-7 Voight St, Windhoek, Namibia
Phone: +264 (0)61 244 347
Email: chameleonbackpackers@iway.na

Website: www.chameleonbackpackers.com
Facebook: www.facebook.com/chameleonsafaris

As it's in the capital, Chameleon BP is a very busy place and you have to reserve beforehand. We didn't and they were fully booked, so we couldn't stay. But it looked like a nice place.

Arebbush Travel Lodge

Coordinates: S22° 36.691' E17° 05.171'
Price: N$125 pp
Address: Cnr of Golf, Auas Road, Olympia, Mandume Ndemufayo Avenue, Windhoek 9000, Namibia
Phone: +264 (0)61 252 255
Email: reservations@arebbusch.com
Website: www.arebbusch.com
Facebook: www.facebook.com/arebbusch

They have two options for campers here: 'luxury' and 'standard'.

Luxury camping means each site has its own shade net and BBQ area.

Standard camping is more of a bush setting, without shade nets and with shared water taps and BBQ areas.

It's a nice campsite. The only minus point is that it's located next to the motorway, so choose a spot as far from the road as possible. They also have a nice restaurant and you can buy wood here, too.

Khorixas

Camping
iGowati Country Lodge

Coordinates: S20° 22.395' E14° 57.913'
Price: N$100 pp
Address: iGowati Country Hotel, PO Box 104, King Justus, Garoëb Avenue, Khorixas, Namibia
Phone 1: +264 (0)67 331 592
Phone 2: +264 (0)67 331 593

It's in a town, next to a road. Nice campsite, but nothing special. We stayed here because we had a flat tyre and were delayed.

Brandberg

Camping
White Lady Lodge

Coordinates: S21° 01.216' E14° 41.361'
Price: N$90 pp and N$30 per car
Phone: +264 (0)64 684 004
Email: ugab@iway.na

Website: www.brandbergwllodge.com
Facebook:
www.facebook.com/pages/Brandberg-White-Lady-Lodge/166778990040211

You pay at the main building, which boasts a bar and pool (and where you can find power points). The camping ground is a bit further; a big, open, sandy area with some trees.

You can see Brandberg from here and watch elephants stroll through the camp! In this region, they have 'desert elephants'. You can take a tour to see them, but if you stay here, they might just come to see you.

Botswana

Our Experience

We didn't spend much time here as we only passed through to visit a friend, so we don't have much to tell you. However, this is the first country where we came into contact with 'biltong' and we can't rave about it enough!

General Information

Capital: Gaborone

Language Spoken: Setswana 78.2%, Kalanga 7.9%, Sekgalagadi 2.8%, English 2.1% (official), other 8.6%, unspecified 0.4% (2001 census)

Population: 2.3 million

Religion: Christian 71.6%, Badimo 6%, other 1.4%, unspecified 0.4%, none 20.6%

Currency: Botswana Pula (BWP)

ATM: Barclays

Electricity: 230V, Type D and G

Climate: Semi-arid, with warm winters and hot summers.

Time Zone: UCT+2

Country Code: +267

Shops: Shoprite

Health: We had our yellow fever certificates checked at the border.

Visa

Cost: Free
Duration: 30 days
Where to Get One: At the border

Travelling by Car

Carnet

When crossing borders within the Southern African Customs Union (South Africa, Namibia, Botswana, Lesoto and Swaziland), you don't need to get your carnet stamped. You only need a stamp upon entering SACU (one of these five countries) and once when you're leaving the customs union with your vehicle.

Costs

Third-Party Insurance: 50 BWP (2013)
Road Permit: 170 BWP (2013)
Road Fund: 50 BWP (2013)

Road Conditions

Lots of Chinese tarmac roads, which means potholes!

Police

We didn't see much of the police here, but there were quite a lot of speed controls en route.

Fuel

No problems getting fuel; diesel and petrol are available, but petrol stations might be far from each other, so best to top up when you get a chance.

Car Help
Landrover Gaborone
> **Address:** Plot 1280, Luthuli Road, Old Industrial Site, Gaborone
> **Phone:** +267 (0)3 972 714
> **Email:** duncan@landrovergabs.co.bw
> **Note:** Official Landrover dealer

Vet Fences
Like Namibia, Botswana uses 'vet fences' to control the spread of animal diseases.

In the north of Botswana, animal diseases are more common and you are not permitted to transport raw meat or animal products (such as unpasteurised milk) from north to south over the 'vet border'.

If you travel from south to north, there is no problem. You are also not permitted to transport meat from west to east, but the opposite direction is not a problem.

At these fences, they will check your car for uncooked meat and animal products. If you would like to take meat over this border, it must be cooked. No raw meat, even if it's frozen or vacuum packed, may be taken over the border.

In Botswana, you are not allowed to transport raw meat from Maun to Nxai Pan, Makgadigadi, Nata or Ghanzi.

You can, however, take meat from Maun to the Tsodillo Hills, Moremi, Chobe and Savuti.

On Tracks4Africa's GPS maps, these fences are referred to as 'vet fences' and are indicated with red lines.

(Source: blog.tracks4africa.co.za/veterinary-fences-in-namibia-and-botswana)

Crossing the Border
Namibia–Botswana
Formalities
Namibian Side
- Fill in exit form.
- Get visa stamped.
- Get carnet stamped if required (see above).

Note: Straightforward and quick

Botswana Side
- Show yellow fever vaccination forms. They will give you a document.
- Fill in the entry form.
- Go to customs with the entry form and yellow fever document.
- They will stamp your visa.
- Fill out the vehicle details. They will give you a document.
- Pay road permit, road fund and insurance fees (see above for prices).
- With the vehicle detail document and carnet, go to customs for the carnet stamp.

Note: You can only bring in 2L of wine per person and 1L spirits per person.

Our Recommendations

Ghanzi

Camping
Jungle Light Rest Camp

Coordinates: S22° 08.388' E020° 51.997'
Price: 75 BWP pp
Address: Kalkfontein, Ghanzi, Botswana
Phone: +267 (0)74 551 504
Email: multigrowth@gmail.com
Facebook: www.facebook.com/pages/Jungle-Light-Rest-Camp/711082438901891

This is the first campsite you will see when you cross the border.

Small, sandy campsite with stone barbecues. There is a little restaurant where the owner makes home-cooked meals.

The campsite is close to the main road, so try to camp as far away from the road as possible.

You can find power points in the restaurant.

Gaborone

Camping
Mokolodi Backpackers

Coordinates: S24° 44.436' E25° 49.667'
Price: 120 BWP pp
Address: Plot 86, Mokolodi, Gaborone, Botswana
Phone: +267 (0)74 111 164
Email: admin@backpackers.co.bw
Website: www.backpackers.co.bw
Facebook:
www.facebook.com/mokolodibackpackers

Camping is slap bang in the middle of this site, so you won't have any privacy, as people will pass your car all the time. There is a swimming pool that's mainly used by the ducks. A (very fat) pig also wanders around.

Lobatse

Camping
Odendaalsrust Farm

Coordinates: S25° 18.933' E25° 36.946'

Price: BWP 100 per person per night
Address: Odendaalsrust Farm, Lobatse district, Botswana
Phone: +267 (0)71 304 897
Email: sharondoepie@gmail.com
Website:
www.lobatseaccommodation.co.za/wmenu.php

We didn't camp here, only bought biltong (which we strongly recommend!). They sell biltong (dried, cured meat) as well as fresh meat here, most of it vacuum-packed so you can keep it for a bit longer.

When we were there, they had a baby giraffe on-site that had lost her mother. A vet was treating her before her transfer to a reserve.

You will easily find the site; look for a big sign depicting a cow that hangs high above the entrance.

South Africa

Our Experience

South Africa is lovely. Its people, its braais, the wine region, the wild nature, the sea … It's not 'real' Africa anymore.

In fact, it's probably the easiest country we've travelled through. There's a lot less hassle here.

We enjoyed much more of a holiday feeling.

We were so glad to finally reach South Africa, as it meant that we made it! But of course, we were also sad to get here.

Our arrival meant the end of our fantastic trans-African adventure.

General Information

Capital: Pretoria, Bloemfontein and Cape Town
Language Spoken: IsiZulu 23.8%, IsiXhosa 17.6%, Afrikaans 13.3%, Sepedi 9.4%, English 8.2%, Setswana 8.2%, Sesotho 7.9%, Xitsonga 4.4%, other 7.2%
Population: 55,338,545 (November 2016)
Religion: Zion Christian 11.1%, Pentecostal/Charismatic 8.2%, Catholic 7.1%, Methodist 6.8%, Dutch Reformed 6.7%, Anglican 3.8%, Muslim 1.5%, other Christian 36%, Other 2.3%, unspecified 1.4%, none 15.1%
Currency: South African Rand
ATM: Almost all ATMs in South Africa accept foreign cards.
Electricity: 220V, Type C, D, M and N
Climate: Mostly semi-arid; subtropical along the East Coast; sunny days, cool nights
Time Zone: UTC +2
Country Code: +27
Shops: Big supermarkets and local markets

Visa

Cost: Free
Duration: 90 days
Where to Get One: At the border

Note

In the past, you could extend your visa by leaving the country and returning a few days later. Unfortunately, the rules have changed since 2015 and this is NOT possible anymore.

Your visa starts counting from the day you enter South Africa and keeps on counting even if you leave and return later.

It is possible to extend your visa, but this is quite expensive and it involves a lot of waiting.

Travelling by Car

Carnet

A carnet is required if you want to ship your vehicle either into or out of South Africa.

When crossing borders within the the boundaries of the Southern African Customs Union (South Africa, Botswana, Namibia, Lesotho and Swaziland), you don't need to get your carnet stamped.

You only need a stamp when first entering one of these countries, or when leaving the customs union.

Car Insurance

N/A

Road Tax
N/A

Road Condition
The best roads we've come across on our travels.

Police
This is the first country where they INSISTED upon looking at our original documents instead of the copies. We didn't have a lot of trouble with the police here. Just remain polite and calm.

Fuel
No problems getting fuel; diesel and petrol are available.

Car Help
Market Toyota Culemborg
> **Address:** Cnr Nelson Mandela Rd & Christiaan Barnard St, Culemborg, CAPE TOWN
> **Phone:** +27 (0)21 410 9300

Imperial Toyota City
> **Address:** 271 Commissioner Street, Jeppestown, JOHANNESBURG
> **Phone:** +27 (0)11 220 4600

Jaguar Landrover
> **Address:** 28 Victoria Link, Route 21 Corporate Park, Nellmapius Drive, Centurion, PRETORIA
> **Phone:** +27 (0)12 450 4000
> **Email:** crcza@jaguarlandrover.com
> **Note:** Official Landrover dealer

Crossing the Border
Botswana–South Africa
Border Used
Lobatse (Botswana)

Formalities
Botswana Side
- Fill out departure form.
- Get exit stamp in passport.
- Check passport when leaving with car.

South African Side
- Get entry stamp in passport.
- Check passport when leaving with car.

Note: Extremely simple and quick. One of the fastest border crossings we've made. It only took 20 minutes.

Our Recommendations

South Africa is a very well-travelled country, both by foreigners and locals, so there are plenty of camping options. However, keep an eye out for school holidays (especially their summer break that runs from the beginning of December until the middle of January). During these holidays, it is VERY hard to find camping spots (especially along the coast) if you haven't made a reservation beforehand. And be warned, prices for camping during this holiday are double!

Try to get your hands on a free copy of 'Coast to Coast'. It's a free booklet listing campsites from all over South Africa. It gives you information about accommodation, prices, things to do, etc. We found it very useful and used it often! You can pick it up in almost any backpacker's haunt. You can also look up accommodations on the Coast to Coast website at www.coasttocoast.co.za.

If you're planning on visiting a lot of national parks, it is worthwhile to consider a 'Wild Card'. With this card, you will have year-long access to the majority of South Africa's national parks. You can buy the card as an individual, as a couple or as a family. For more information, go to www.wildcard.co.za.

Kimberley

Things to See

Big Hole

This is the biggest man-made hole in the world. Have a look at this spectacular place, watch a movie about the mine and have a stroll through the adjoining mining town museum. Open from Monday to Sunday, 08:00 a.m. to 05:00 p.m.

Entrance Fees:
    Adult: R100
    Child: R60 (4 to 12 Years)

Camping

Big Hole Caravan Park

    Coordinates: S28° 44.386' E24° 75.180'
    Price: R76 per person per night
    Address: 10 West Circular Road, Kimberley,

Northern Cape, 8301, South Africa
Phone: +27 (0)53 830 6322
Website: www.campsa.co.za/bighole

Not amazing. It's a grassy fenced area close to the 'Big Hole', but it's next to a big car park, so people can watch you through the fence. Convenient if you want to visit Big Hole in the morning. They have braais available.

Bloemfontein

Camping

Reyneke Caravan Park

Coordinates: S29° 07.739' E26° 09.403'
Price: R250 per campsite accommodating 1–4 persons.
Address: 5B Brendar Road, Kwaggafontein, Bloemfontein, 9301, South Africa
Phone: +27 (0)51 523 3888
Email: info@reynekepark.co.za
Website: www.reynekepark.co.za
Facebook: www.facebook.com/pages/Reyneke Park /257548544256402?rf=29173641750813

Nice, grassy area with trees for shade. There are also some braai areas and a little shop on-site.

Stutterheim

Camping
The Shire Eco Lodge

Coordinates: S32° 32.253' E27° 23.050'
Price: R60 pp
Address: 6 km (4 miles) from Stutterheim in the Eastern Cape Province of South Africa.
Phone: +27 (0)43 683 2452
Email: rob@shire.co.za
Website: www.shire.co.za

This place is so beautiful. They have the cutest little cottages and a lovely camping ground. When we were there, we were the only ones on the huge, grassy plot slap bang in the middle of the surrounding nature. You can also go on some lovely walks through the bush and up the hill.

Wild Lubanzi

Coordinates: S32° 04.085' E29° 05.154'
Price: R80 pp
Phone: +27 (0)78 530 8997
Email: wild@lubanzi.co.za
Website: www.wildlubanzi.co.za

Beautiful spot!

Very high up, so you can look down at the ocean and watch waves breaking on the cliff. It can get very windy up here and we were told to avoid putting up our rooftop tent, so we slept in a room (at extra cost).

The road up here is a bit rough and can get slippery when wet, but it's nothing a 4WD can't handle.

Vaalwater

Things to See
The Kruger National Park
The Kruger National Park, with its two million hectares of territory, is probably the most visited park in South Africa.

It's easy to access and is a wonderful place for self-drive safaris.

There are plenty of camps dotted through the park where you can pitch your tent after a day of wildlife spotting.

Make sure you're at the campsite before sundown, because at sundown all the gates closes, and it's time for the animals to rule over the place!

You can camp in the park itself and you have the choice between the main campsites, where there are restaurants, a shop, a pool, electricity, etc. and bush campsites, which are a bit more basic.

All the campsites can be booked online at <u>www.sanparks.org/parks/kruger/camps</u>.

Camping
Olievenhoutsrus

Price: R150 pp
Address: 33, Vaalwater, 0530, South Africa
Phone: +27 (0)14 755 4441
Email: olievenhoutsrus@lantic.net
Website: www.vaalwateraccommodation.co.za
Facebook:
www.facebook.com/pages/Olievenhoutsrus-Guest-Game-Farm-Vaalwater/103230616380837

Another wonderful place to stay! Very nice and relaxed, with a swimming pool and a big kitchen/lounge area.

You can go out for a walk to spot the wildlife, but if you're too lazy, they put food out in the evening and the animals come of their own accord (on the other side of the fence, though).

Kelso

Camping
Happy Wanderers

Coordinates: S30° 21.264' E30° 43.056'
Price: R300 for two persons, R400 for two persons

on weekends.

Address: 1 Abrams Drive, Kelso, 4183, KZN. 4180 Kelso Beach, Kwazulu-Natal, South Africa
Phone: +27 (0)39 975 1104
Email: happywanderers@telkomsa.net
Website: www.happywanderers.co.za
Facebook: www.facebook.com/pages/Happy-Wanderers-Holiday-Resort/148362078570575

Nice campsite along the beach, but pricey! Can get very crowded during school holidays. Wi-Fi in the bar.

Hluhluwe

Camping
Bush Baby Lodge

Coordinates: S28° 04.923' E32° 17.492'
Price: R110 pp
Phone: +27 (0)76 953 7063
Email: bushbaby@101fc.nl
Website: www.bushbabylodge.co.za
Facebook: www.facebook.com/pages/Bushbaby-Lodge/147176765353852

Nice campsite, with an outdoor kitchen and a swimming pool.

They put food out at night for the bush babies.

Pongola

Things to See
Pongola Game Reserve
Coordinates: S27° 26.798' E31° 53.425'

We went to this reserve because there were twin baby elephants born here at the end of 2014. As the chance of an elephant having twins is only 1%, we wanted to see them! So we went on an 'Elephant Tour' and it was amazing. We were the only people there and Heike, the woman in charge of the elephants, took us on a drive to search for the twins. We thought we would drive for about an hour, see the elephants and go back. However, we ended up spending more than three hours searching, looking around and taking pictures.

Heike is so passionate about her job, so it's a pleasure to go on a tour with her. She is not there to profit from the tourists and take them for a ten-minute tour; she wants you to enjoy the elephants as much as she does. She helps you to track an elephant on your own (with an antenna), gives you a book to see how you can recognise which elephant is which and is more than happy to answer all of your questions. It was such a lovely experience which we thoroughly recommend!

You can book tours through White Elephant Lodge.

Details:

Email: whiteelephant@xsinet.co.za
Phone: +27(0)34 435 1012
Price for Elephant Tour: R350 pp
Entry per Car: R20

Camping
Sodwana Angling Club

Coordinates: S27° 19.337' E31° 53.658'
Price: R40 pp
Address: Simdlangenthsha, Pongola, KwaZulu-Natal, ZA
Phone: +27 (0)34 413 2256
Email: ina@sodwanahengelklub.co.za
Website:
www.sodwanahengelklub.co.za/Home.htm

This is a nice, quiet campsite where local people come to go fishing. We stayed here because it was the cheapest option near the Pongola Game Reserve.

Sodwana Bay

Camping
Maak 'n Jol

> **Coordinates:** S27° 30.729' E32° 39.383'
> **Price:** R100 per person per day
> **Address:** 1D Sodwana Bay Rd, Mbazwana, South Africa
> **Phone:** +27 (0)35 571 0165
> **Email:** maak.n.jol@mweb.co.za

Nice, large camping spots, but the campsite can get crowded during the school holidays. They have a really nice bar and if you want a night out, you should have one here! The bar can get a bit noisy (especially on weekends), so ask for a plot on the other side of the camping grounds. If you're not into parties, there are plenty of lovely, calmer campsites in Sodwana Bay.

Warner Beach

Camping
Blue Sky Mining Backpackers

Price: R100 pp out of season, R120 pp in season
Address: 5 Nelson Palmer Road, Kingsburg (30min south of Durban)
Phone 1: +27 (0)83 713 9896
Phone 2: +27 (0)83 733 6468
Email: bsm1@mweb.co.za
Website: www.blueskymining.co.za

This is a backpacker's haven, but the campsite is on the other side of the compound, behind the kitchen, so you will be far from the rooms and the bar. Both the bar and the restaurant are nice. The beach is on the other side of the road.

Drakensberg

Camping
Amphitheatre Backpackers

Coordinates: S28° 38.601' E29° 09.543'
Price: R85 per person per night
Address: R74, Northern Drakensberg. The route description can be found on the website.
Phone: +27 (0)82 855 9767
Email: amphibackpackers@worldonline.co.za
Website: amphibackpackers.co.za
Facebook:
www.facebook.com/
AmphitheatreBackpackersLodge

This camping ground is in a beautiful setting! A big, grassy area far enough away from the camp buildings. They celebrate the New Year with a big, three-day festival.

Ikhaya Lodge

Coordinates: S28° 58.059' E29° 26.815'
Price: R600 per night for two people
Address: Bergvlei FarmBell Park dam road, 4 Winterton, 3340, KZN South Africa
Phone: +27 (0)72 312 2659
Email: ikhayalodge@hotmail.com
Website: www.monkscowl.com

Small campsite in a beautiful setting!

You can go horse riding here. Just amazing!

Cintsa West

Camping
Buccaneers Backpackers

Coordinates: S32° 50.162' E28° 06.592'
Price: R100 pp
Address: Cintsa West, 5217 Cintsa, Eastern Cape, South Africa
Phone: +27 (0)43 734 3012
Email: buccaneers@cintsa.com
Website: www.cintsa.com
Facebook: www.facebook.com/pages/Buccaneers-Backpackers/149736731712162

Another stunning campsite close to the beach. Like other holiday spots, it can get crowded during school holidays. The way up to the site is a bit steep. Make sure you use your 4WD switch when it rains! Delicious, free breakfast along with free activities every evening and, to top it all, it's close to the ocean.

Cape St Francis

Things to See
Penguin Rehab Centre
Coordinates: S34° 12.728' E24° 50.202'

Nice place to stop if you're passing by. They take care of injured penguins here and release them back to the wild.

You can see the penguins through a window when they go swimming in their own private pool, or watch them wandering around outside in their enclosure. They also do private behind the scenes tours.

You can adopt and name one of the penguins, too. This money is used to fund penguin treatment and the penguins' release costs.

Nature Valley

Camping
Wild Spirit

Coordinates: S33° 56.889' E23° 31.262'
Price: R100 pp
Address: R102, Nature's Valley Road, The Crags
Phone: +27 (0)82 828 8008
Email: info@wildspiritlodge.co.za
Website: www.wildspiritlodge.co.za

Nice, big, grassy campsite between the trees. They have a really lovely bar/restaurant overlooking the forest. You can also go for a walk in the forest. The trail will take you to a little waterfall, where you can take a refreshing dip. Electricity and Wi-Fi is available in the restaurant.

Montagu

Camping
De Bos Guest Farm

> **Coordinates:** S33° 47.323' E20° 06.779'
> **Price:** R80 pp
> **Address:** 8 Brown Street, 6720 Montagu, Western Cape
> **Phone:** +27 (0)23 614 2532
> **Email:** info@debos.co.za
> **Website:** www.debos.co.za
> **Facebook:** www.facebook.com/debosguestfarm

A small, nice, quiet campsite between the trees. We stopped here as we wanted to meet up with a friend. If you do decide to stay here, there is a great Irish pub nearby.

Things to See and Do

We were originally convinced there was nothing to do in Montagu, but our South African editor (who used to live near Montagu) offered to give us a few suggestions of things you might want to try while you're here.

Avalon Springs
www.avalonsprings.co.za/day-visitors.php

Go for a swim in the natural hot springs and enjoy their 60-metre-long water slide.

They work on a first-come-first-serve basis and close the gate once there are 300 people in the resort, so go early, especially on holidays.

> **Prices**
> **Weekday (outside school holiday):** R55 pp
> **Weekend (outside school holiday):** R100 pp
> **School Vacations, Long Weekends, Public Holidays:** R120 pp

Explore the Route 62
www.route62.co.za

Montagu is on the Route 62, which is famous for its gorgeous scenery, its wine and its cultural activities. It's well worth a road trip to explore the towns on this route.

If you follow the road towards Cape Town, you can taste some of the most interesting New World wines South Africa has to offer. Or if you want to escape into another world altogether, go in the opposite direction to Oudtshoorn, where you can tour the Cango Caves.

Oudtshoorn is also home to South Africa's biggest and oldest arts festival. It's a must-see if you want to experience the local (Afrikaans) culture, but if you want to avoid crowds, give Oudtshoorn a skip on and the week before Easter.

There's a lot to do and enjoy along Route 62, and our editor highly reccommends you simply take a drive along the route and stop by the tourism office of each town to see what strikes your fancy, as outlining all the activities town-by-town will take another book all of its own.

Swellendam
Swellendam is a picturesque little town in the mountains,

and is in fact the third oldest town in South Africa, after Cape Town and Stellenbosch. It's worth a trip to see the beautiful old buildings and to visit the fantastic museums and historic buildings there.

But arguably the best thing about going to Swellendam from Montagu is the scenery. This trip takes you through the Tradouw Pass, which cuts through the mountains between Montagu and Swellendam. It's not a challenging route, but it's almost impossible to drive through this pass without stopping at least once to admire the scenery that seems to change to a new postcard image with every turn.

If you don't want to take a trip only to Swellendam, you can go on to Cape Aghullas, which according to our editor is a better day-trip than travelling there from Stellenbosch.

Stellenbosch

Things to See and Do
Cape Agulhas
Coordinates: S34° 83.313' E19° 99.998'

The most southerly point of Africa.

Camping
African Overlanders

> **Coordinates:** S33° 52.300' E18° 44.088'
> **Price:** R70 pp, kids under 12 free
> **Address:** Two Hoots Farm, Koopmans Kloof Farm, Stellenbosch Farms, Botfontein Road, Western Cape, SA 7570
> **Phone:** +27 (0)71 521 9742
> **Email:** africanoverlanders@live.com
> **Website:** www.africanoverlanders.com

This is the place to be if you need help with your car or if you want to ship your car out. Duncan used to be an overlander himself and has been helping out travellers for years. It's a nice, quiet campsite, but hard to find! There is a quite good road description on his website. There is pretty decent internet on the campsite and hot showers, if you shower when the sun shines.

West Coast

Camping
Leentjeklip Caravan Park

Coordinates: S33° 03.945' E18° 02.493'
Price: R119/stand and R143/seaside stand
Address: Langebaan, Saldanha Bay, West Coast, South Africa
Phone: +27 (0)22 772 2461
Website:
www.saldanhabay.co.za/pages/resorts/Leentjiesklip/leentjies.html

Campsite beside the sea.

Melkbosstrand

Camping
Ou Skip

Price: R110/stand
Address: 1 Otto du Plessis Drive, Melkbosstrand, 7441, Western Cape, South Africa
Phone: +27 (0)21 553 2058
Email: ouskip@intekom.co.za
Website: www.ouskip.co.za

Big, grassy campsite with most plots separated by hedging.

Swaziland

Our Experience

There is a world of difference between Swaziland and South Africa! Swaziland is a lot more 'real Africa' than South Africa is; it's beautiful and green. Piggs Peak is simply a must!

There are little stone carvers along the way up to Piggs Peak who produce the most beautiful figures out of stone. These stone carvers love to swap stuff, as it's such a long walk (uphill or down) to the shops.

If you have a spare T-shirt, towel, bottle of water or even an apple, they will be more than happy to exchange what you have for one of their beautiful carvings.

People in Swaziland are still relatively new to tourism, so people tend to be a lot more honest which, as far as we are concerned, is just lovely.

General Information

Capital: Mbabane

Language Spoken: English (official, government business conducted in English), siSwati (official)

Population: 1 314 741 (November 2016)

Religion: Zionist (a blend of Christianity and indigenous ancestral worship) 40%, Roman Catholic 20%, Muslim 10%, other (includes Anglican, Baha'i, Methodist, Mormon, Jewish) 30%

Currency: Lilangeni, but South African Rand (R) is also accepted. The value is the same.

ATM: Standard Bank

Electricity: 220V, Type D

Climate: Varies from tropical to near temperate.

Time Zone: GMT +2

Country Code: +268

Shops: Spar and informal markets

Visa

A visa is not required for visitors from most countries if they'll be in the country for fewer than 30 days.

Travelling by Car

Carnet

When crossing borders within the boundaries of the Southern African Customs Union (Botswana, Namibia, South Africa, Lesotho and Swaziland), you don't need to get your carnet stamped. You only need a stamp when entering or leaving SACU.

Car Insurance

Third-party insurance, which is included in the fuel price.

Road Tax

R50

Road Condition

Mainly tarmac roads.

Police

We never came across any police.

Fuel

Available in larger towns.

Crossing the Border

South Africa–Swaziland

Border Used

Lavumisa

Info

It's a very easy and quick crossing.

Formalities
South African Side
- You will receive a gate pass when you enter the border. Keep it.
- Get passport stamped.
- Give the gate pass back.

Swaziland Side
- You get another gate pass.
- Passport stamped.
- Pay for temporary import permit.
- Car inspection.
- Give the gate pass back.

Swaziland–South Africa
Border Used
Bulembu

Info
Very easy and quick crossing, but the border closes at 4 p.m. so make sure you're there at least 30 minutes beforehand, as you will have to drive for a bit between Swaziland customs and South African customs. We arrived at 3:55 p.m. and we got through Swaziland customs. When we arrived at the South African customs, they had already locked their gates, leaving us stuck in no man's land.

We saw the officer closing the gate and we know he had seen us as we were driving right towards him, but he hurriedly locked the gate and rushed to the main building. We jumped out of the car and started yelling. He carried on walking, acting as if he couldn't hear us (did he really plan on leaving us there in no man's land for the night?), but at last, he turned around and came to open the gate for us.

Formalities

Swaziland Side
- Get visa stamped.
- Drive to the South African side (500 meters of zigzagging road, uphill).

South African Side
- Get visa stamped.

Our Recommendations

Things to See

Ngwenya Glass

Here, they are experts at glass blowing and you can go up some stairs and look down to see how the glass is blown. It's really impressive. They also have a shop where you can buy some beautiful, locally blown glass.

Entry: Free
Website: www.ngwenyaglass.co.sz

Piggs Peak

This is an absolute must, it's so, SO beautiful! All along the way, you will find plenty of places to stop to admire the view, most of them giving you information about the road, the hills and the history of the region. You will find the stone carvers along this road, too.

Lobamba

Camping
Legends Backpackers

Coordinates: S26° 26.407' E31° 10.988'
Price: R80 per person per night

Address: Mantenga Falls Road, 1, H106, Swaziland
Email: info@legends.co.sz
Phone: +268 (0)24 161 870
Mobile: +268 (0)76 020 261
Website: www.legends.co.sz
Facebook: www.facebook.com/Legends.Swaziland

This is a nice backpacker's place where camping spots are placed between the trees, away from the buildings. Electricity is available in the kitchen.

Lesotho

Our Experience

Due to poor time management on our side, we only spent two days in Lesotho. We might not have seen much, but what we did see was really worth the effort! We drove up the Sani Pass and WOW! That was incredible! We also grabbed a beer at the highest pub in Africa, so life couldn't really have been better.

General Information

Capital: Maseru
Language Spoken: Sesotho (Southern Sotho), English (official), Zulu, Xhosa
Population: 2,155,464
Religion: Christian 80%, indigenous beliefs 20%
Currency: Loti, but South African Rand is also accepted. The value is the same.
ATM: ATMs that accept foreign bank cards can only be found in Maseru, so bring money before entering.
Electricity: 220V, South African/Indian three round pin, Type D
Climate: Temperate; cool to cold, with dry winters and hot, wet summers
Time Zone: UTC +2
Country Code: +266
Shops: Supermarkets and local markets

Visa

Cost: Free
Validity: 30 days
Where to Get One: At the border

Travelling by Car

Carnet

No need to get your carnet stamped, as you're already in the Southern African Customs Union.

Car Insurance

N/A

Road Tax
R60

Road condition
Sand/dirt

Police
Never bumped into them.

Fuel
Available in the big cities.

Crossing the Border
South Africa–Lesotho
Border Used
Sani Pass border

Info
Very easy and quick. They didn't even bother checking our passport photos.

Formalities
South African Side
- At the bottom of the Sani Pass, you will be given an exit stamp.
- Drive up the entire length of the Sani Pass. (BEAUTIFUL!)

Lesotho Side
- Receive an entry stamp at the top of the Sani Pass and pay R60 road tax.

Our Recommendations

Unfortunately, we only stayed in Lesotho for one night.

Sani Pass

Things to Do
Sani Pass
This is an absolute must—it's so, so, so beautiful! It's a steep climb, but nothing a 4WD can't handle. Keep an eye out for the weather. When we drove up, we had beautiful clear skies. When we went down again, it was very cloudy and rainy and we couldn't see the stunning views. It was also quite muddy and slippery.

Have a Beer

Have a beer at the highest pub in Africa! As soon as you reach the top of the Sani Pass and have gone through customs, you will see Sani Mountain Lodge on your right. Order a beer and look out over the Sani Pass. As soon as the sun sets, you will see the clouds rolling towards you and, in no time at all, you will be sitting with your head in the clouds—literally!

Camping
Sani Top Campsite

Coordinates: S29° 34.927' E29° 17.052'
Price: R95
Address: Sani Pass, Sani Pass, Lesotho
Phone: +27 (0)78 634 7496
Website: www.sanimountain.co.za
Facebook:
https://www.facebook.com/Sani-Mountain-Lodge-Sani-Top-636799083121051/

You can camp outside the backpackers building and use the kitchen inside. As you're so high up, it can be BLOODY cold and foggy as soon as the sun sets! You pay at Sani Mountain Lodge, where they have free Wi-Fi if you want it.

Acknowledgements

Writing this book was a horrible experience. Seriously, if you ever think about writing a book, think twice. It takes AGES!

But it's finally finished and I'm very proud of it!

During our travels, we lost some people very close to us, including our beloved grandparents. We would therefore love to dedicate this book to them, as they were the ones who told us to go and not stay home just to be close to them. They told us to follow our dreams. So we left on our travels and very sadly missed the last few months/years of their lives.

We know you were proud of us and, although we were far away, we thought of you all the time.

I also want to thank the rest of both of our families, including my family genes, which I must have inherited, seeing as I also have the urge to travel travel travel! And I want to thank my partner's genes too, for giving him the courage to follow me into such a crazy adventure.

Of course, we can't forget our parents for their support, their help in times of need and their belief in us. Because if there is one thing you can't do without, it is having people who believe in you. It has been an amazing adventure, but at times, it also had its share of loneliness and hardship, and some days, yes, we wanted to give up. But then an email would arrive from mum, or we'd get a text from a friend, or someone would post us something on Facebook ... It might have been a small gesture for them, but to us, it made a world of a difference.

And I couldn't have finished this book without the help of a few awesome women who helped me with this book! Thanks Misha, Sarah and Suzan for your hard work, the book looks amazing!

Oh, and not to forget my partner Dries, who continuously encouraged me to 'finish that freaking book'. Thanks hun, it's finished.

And last but not least, thanks, Mister Carrot, for sticking with us for all of these years, through drought, rain, freezing cold, sweltering heat, storms, hikes, dives ... We're very surprised but so incredibly happy that you survived.

Oh, and one very very final but very very important dedication. Thank YOU! Thank you for reading this book, which (hopefully) means you bought it. Part of this book's profits will go to the Rhino Fund Uganda.

So thank you for supporting both us *and* the rhinos!

Love,

Eef

Get in Touch

Do you think something is missing in the book or did you find a big error?

Please let us know!

Also, if you would like some more specific information that you couldn't find in the book, feel free to contact us. We're more than happy to help!

> **Email:** info@intoafrica.be
> **Facebook:** www.facebook.com/WaarIsWorteltje

To see some real action from our trip, find us on YouTube at Where Is Mister Carrot, or go straight to www.youtube.com/channel/UC05j6htkVJbzufOzYQWG2-Q.

For more pictures and stories, you can also have a look at our website www.whereismistercarrot.com.

Printed by Amazon Italia Logistica S.r.l.
Torrazza Piemonte (TO), Italy

11410125R00215